THE SHAME OF IRANIAN HUMAN RIGHTS

JOINT HEARING

BEFORE THE

SUBCOMMITTEE ON AFRICA, GLOBAL HEALTH, GLOBAL HUMAN RIGHTS, AND INTERNATIONAL ORGANIZATIONS

AND THE

SUBCOMMITTEE ON THE MIDDLE EAST AND NORTH AFRICA

OF THE

COMMITTEE ON FOREIGN AFFAIRS HOUSE OF REPRESENTATIVES

ONE HUNDRED FOURTEENTH CONGRESS

FIRST SESSION

FEBRUARY 26, 2015

Serial No. 114–16

Printed for the use of the Committee on Foreign Affairs

Available via the World Wide Web: http://www.foreignaffairs.house.gov/ or http://www.gpo.gov/fdsys/

U.S. GOVERNMENT PUBLISHING OFFICE

93–535PDF   WASHINGTON : 2015

For sale by the Superintendent of Documents, U.S. Government Publishing Office
Internet: bookstore.gpo.gov   Phone: toll free (866) 512–1800; DC area (202) 512–1800
Fax: (202) 512–2104   Mail: Stop IDCC, Washington, DC 20402–0001

COMMITTEE ON FOREIGN AFFAIRS

EDWARD R. ROYCE, California, *Chairman*

CHRISTOPHER H. SMITH, New Jersey
ILEANA ROS-LEHTINEN, Florida
DANA ROHRABACHER, California
STEVE CHABOT, Ohio
JOE WILSON, South Carolina
MICHAEL T. McCAUL, Texas
TED POE, Texas
MATT SALMON, Arizona
DARRELL E. ISSA, California
TOM MARINO, Pennsylvania
JEFF DUNCAN, South Carolina
MO BROOKS, Alabama
PAUL COOK, California
RANDY K. WEBER SR., Texas
SCOTT PERRY, Pennsylvania
RON DeSANTIS, Florida
MARK MEADOWS, North Carolina
TED S. YOHO, Florida
CURT CLAWSON, Florida
SCOTT DesJARLAIS, Tennessee
REID J. RIBBLE, Wisconsin
DAVID A. TROTT, Michigan
LEE M. ZELDIN, New York
TOM EMMER, Minnesota

ELIOT L. ENGEL, New York
BRAD SHERMAN, California
GREGORY W. MEEKS, New York
ALBIO SIRES, New Jersey
GERALD E. CONNOLLY, Virginia
THEODORE E. DEUTCH, Florida
BRIAN HIGGINS, New York
KAREN BASS, California
WILLIAM KEATING, Massachusetts
DAVID CICILLINE, Rhode Island
ALAN GRAYSON, Florida
AMI BERA, California
ALAN S. LOWENTHAL, California
GRACE MENG, New York
LOIS FRANKEL, Florida
TULSI GABBARD, Hawaii
JOAQUIN CASTRO, Texas
ROBIN L. KELLY, Illinois
BRENDAN F. BOYLE, Pennsylvania

AMY PORTER, *Chief of Staff*   THOMAS SHEEHY, *Staff Director*
JASON STEINBAUM, *Democratic Staff Director*

(II)

CONTENTS

THE SHAME OF IRANIAN HUMAN RIGHTS

THURSDAY, FEBRUARY 26, 2015

House of Representatives,
Subcommittee on Africa, Global Health,
Global Human Rights, and International Organizations and
Subcommittee on the Middle East and North Africa,
Committee on Foreign Affairs,
Washington, DC.

The committees met, pursuant to notice, at 2 o'clock p.m., in room 2172 Rayburn House Office Building, Hon. Christopher H. Smith (chairman of the Subcommittee on Africa, Global Health, Global Human Rights, and International Organizations) presiding.

Mr. SMITH. The subhearing of the joint subcommittees will come to order, and good afternoon to everybody.

At a time when the administration seems keen to reach a nuclear accord that relies at least to some extent on trust, although there are some verification aspects to it, with the Iranian regime and perhaps even a de facto collaboration in the fight against ISIS, it is wise to consider and scrutinize the dismal human rights record of this country which we are currently conducting negotiations with.

How they treat their own people is illustrative of how they see and will treat outsiders. This hearing provides a critical examination of human rights in Iran, which is important and necessary in its own right, and also places in context the administration's efforts toward a nuclear deal.

According to the report by the U.N. Special Rapporteur on Human Rights in Iran, between July 2013 and June 2014, at least 852 people were executed in Iran. Shockingly, some of those executed were children under the age of 18. Iranian human rights activists place the number of people executed by the regime at 1,181.

The current Department of State human rights report states that Iranian human rights violations include disappearances; cruel, inhuman, or degrading treatment; mistreatment of prisoners including judicially sanctioned amputation and flogging; rape; politically motivated violence and repression; harsh and life-threatening conditions in detention and prison facilities, with instances of death in custody; arbitrary arrests and lengthy pretrial detention, sometimes incommunicado.

While the Iranian Constitution grants equal rights to all ethnic minorities and allows for minority languages to be used in the media and in schools, minorities do not enjoy equal rights and the regime consistently denies their right to use their language in school. In addition, a 1985 law prohibits non-Shi'a ethnic minorities from fully participating in civic life. That law and its associated provisions make full access of employment, education and other areas conditional on a devotion to the Islamic Republic and the tenets of the Shi'a Islam.

The regime disproportionately targets minority groups including Kurds, Arabs, Azeris, and others, for arbitrary arrest, prolonged detention, and physical abuse. These groups report political and socioeconomic discrimination particularly in their access to economic aid, business licenses, university admissions, permission to publish books, and housing and land rights.

Because of the severe religious freedom abuses, our Government has designated Iran as a Country of Particular Concern since 1999, each year. Frequently, the arrest and harassment of members of religious minorities has continued following a significant increase in 2012. The government severely restricts religious freedom, and there have been reports of imprisonment, harassment, intimidation, and discrimination based on those faith beliefs.

There has been continued reports of government charging religious and ethnic minorities with ''enmity against God,'' ''anti-Islamic propaganda,'' or vague national security crimes for their religious activities. Those reportedly arrested on religious grounds face poor prison conditions and treatment, as with most prisoners of conscience.

One of the imprisoned on religious grounds is Pastor Saeed Abedini, a U.S. citizen and father of two—Rebekkah and Jacob—and a Christian imprisoned in Iran because of his, and only because of, his faith. Pastor Abedini was imprisoned by the Iranian regime nearly 1,000 days ago when members of the Revolutionary Guard pulled him off a bus and then placed him under house arrest. He later was taken away in chains to Evin prison, where he endured periods of solitary confinement, beatings, internal bleeding, death threats, and continued psychological torture all because he would not deny his Christian faith.

What was Pastor Abedini's crime? According to the court, he was a threat to the security of Iran because of his leadership role in Christian churches between 2000 and 2005. And I would note parenthetically that he was allowed to go back to build an orphanage, got the approval and then had that all reversed and then he was arrested.

President Obama promised Pastor Abedini's son Jacob that he would do all he can to gain his father's release by the boy's birthday next month. Yesterday, the Secretary of State in answer to a question I posed said the administration was working quietly to gain Pastor Abedini's release as soon as possible. Let us hope.

Meanwhile, Iran is repeatedly cited for virtually unrelenting repression of the Baha'is community which Iran's Shiite Muslim clergy views as a heretical sect. Baha'is number about 300,000–350,000. At least 30 Baha'i remained imprisoned and 60 were arrested in 2012. A February 2013 U.N. report said that 110 Baha'is were in jail. They had said that 133 were expected to start serving jail time.

Since the 1979 Islamic Revolution, the regime has executed more than 200 Baha'is simply because of their faith. The regime frequently prevents many Baha'is from leaving the country, harasses them, persecutes them, and generally disregards their property rights. I would note parenthetically that when Ronald Reagan was President and was the first one to raise the issue at the Presidential level, I was there at the White House when he so designated the defense of the Baha'i as a very vital, important interest of the United States and all concerned about human rights.

Iranian courts offer no recourse to the monstrous violations of human rights because without an independent judiciary Iranians and foreigners tied to those courts are routinely denied fair trials sometimes resulting in executions without due process.

I'd like to now yield to Mr. Deutch for any opening comments he may have.

Mr. DEUTCH. Thank you. Thank you Chairman Smith, Chairman Ros-Lehtinen and Ranking Member Bass for holding today's joint hearing. It is very important that our two subcommittees come together today to shine a light on Iran's atrocious human rights record. And I apologize because this is an issue I care deeply about but I'm going to be running back and forth to another hearing taking place at the same time.

While the world anxiously awaits to see what if any agreement will be reached on Iran's nuclear weapons program, this hearing serves as an important reminder that even beyond the dangerous and illicit program Iran's regime routinely violates human rights of the Iranian people. At the same time that the news is focused on Geneva, back in Iran the human rights situation is as dismal as ever.

We are well past the Ahmadinejad period in Iran where inflammatory statements made criticism easy. Enough time has passed to see what the Rouhani administration can do. Unfortunately it appears that Rouhani has fallen short on many of his campaign promises, hamstrung perhaps by the Supreme Leader's ultimate and absolute control. The Iranian economy continues to suffer due to the intransigence of its leaders, and the Iranian people remain repressed and restricted by the ultra-conservative social policies of the Ayatollah.

Today's hearing serves as an important reminder that even if we were to resolve the nuclear issue, even if hypothetically the P5+1 reaches an acceptable nuclear deal, Iran still remains a global leader in terrorism financing and human rights abuses. Iran would still be willing to sentence a juvenile to death for the crime of corruption on earth and imprison hundreds of political prisoners.

This is a government that refuses for its own people some of the most fundamental human rights, a government that is willing to perpetuate misogynistic, racist, and homophobic policies, and one that will relentlessly defend its right to possess nuclear capabilities while the Supreme Leader continues to decry Israel's right to simply exist.

Showing a complete disregard for the principle of the right to life, Iran continues to execute its citizens at alarming rates. Official sources put the number of executions in 2014 at 200, but the actual number could likely be over 700. Many of those individuals were charged with questionable or vague offenses, like a woman last October that was convicted of killing a man that she claimed was in the act of raping her. With dozens and dozens of offenses that carry capital punishment, Iran's judiciary has shown just how easy it is for an individual to be put to death, with over 80 Iranians executed in January of this year alone.

The government allows no room for political dissent or critical belief. The regime continues to censor journalists and political activists and to deny its citizens their freedom of speech and opinion. Iran's unfounded arrest and subsequent jailing of Washington Post journalist Jason Rezaian on trumped up charges is despicable and must be condemned by all responsible nations.

The Internet is certainly not an open and safe space in Iran. Anything from a Facebook post to a viral video can land an individual in jail for years. And with one of the highest incarceration rates in the world, Iran certainly exercises their willingness to imprison individuals in order to keep absolute control over media and news content consumed by the people.

Another favorite tactic of the Iranian regime is targeting ethnic and religious minorities. The country's largest non-Muslim religious minority, people of the Baha'i Faith, face particularly hostile treatment. This community is denied freedom of religion, they live under constant fear of arrest, attacks, and destruction of their religious sites. Over 100 Baha'is are currently held in detention and many international reports have criticized Iran's failure to ensure that they receive a fair trial and adequate access to counsel.

Many other groups also face bigotry and targeted discrimination. Christians and Sunni Muslims, Arabs, Kurds, and Azeris, and many more religious and ethnic minority groups are also frequently targeted by the regime, and many are forced to hide signs of their identity while in public.

Women are still subservient to men in many aspects of daily life, and as we witnessed from the gruesome pictures of acid attacks last fall, women are still targeted for violating social norms as set by the state's religious interpretations.

For the LGBT community the environment in Iran is bleak. LGBT individuals face discrimination from their government but also from their friends and families. They can't turn to the courts because same-sex relationships are criminalized. They can't report attacks to law enforcement authorities out of fear that they may be arrested for being LGBT.

And there's little information or support available on the ground. The head of Iran's human rights council made the government's position clear when he said that universal human rights should not be extended to what he referred to as the homosexual lifestyle.

Yesterday during another Foreign Affairs Committee hearing, I implored Secretary Kerry to continue to raise the case of Bob Levinson, an American citizen and my constituent, who has been missing in Iran since March 2007, while our negotiators sit across the table from the Iranians. Eight years later Bob is still not home. Despite indications by the Iranian Government of their willingness to assist in this case, we're nearing the eighth anniversary of his disappearance and we see no positive signs. We must continue to advocate for help in Bob's case and for the release of the other American citizens unjustly held in Iran, Amir Hekmati and Pastor Abedini.

Last November we passed a resolution condemning the Iranian Government for these and many more human rights violations, a long list to be sure, but it is important that we as a body consistently condemn these policies and practices. Unfortunately the same is not the case for the rest of the world. The U.N. General Assembly's Third Committee also voted last fall in a resolution on Iran's human rights abuses. And while it passed with 78 votes, 69 countries abstained and 35 countries voted against it.

Finally, as we get closer to the deadlines for negotiations with Iran, I urge my colleagues in Congress and our negotiators in Geneva to not take our eyes off what is happening on the ground in Iran. With such deplorable human rights abuses occurring daily and millions of Iranians repressed and facing discrimination, we've got to keep the global spotlight on Iran and condemn the government's disregard for basic human rights. That is what today's hearing will do.

I want to thank again the chairman. I want to thank our witnesses. I look forward to hearing from you today.

Mr. SMITH. Thank you very much, Mr. Deutch.

It is a privilege to join Ileana Ros-Lehtinen, the former chairman of the full committee and now chairman of the Subcommittee on the Middle East and North Africa. This is both of our subcommittees' joint hearing. I yield to my good friend and colleague.

Ms. ROS-LEHTINEN. Thank you so much, Chairman Smith, and thank you for holding this joint subcommittee hearing on this important topic. And in fact this is the third hearing that Chairman Smith and I have held on the issue of human rights in Iran, and I am appreciative of your continued dedicated leadership on this issue.

I want to first start with some good news. We confirmed yesterday that Rozita Vaseghi was finally released last month after a 5-year sentence in prison in Iran. Rozita is a member of the persecuted Baha'i community that you have heard about from my colleagues. They are Iran's largest non-Muslim religious minority and I adopted her as a prisoner of conscience last year as part of the Tom Lanto Human Rights Commission's Defending Freedoms project.

And while I am relieved, all of us are, that Rozita has been released and will be able to get the health care that she needs after years of brutal mistreatment and solitary confinement, we know that her ordeal is not over. She has not been given any paperwork. Authorities have not told her whether she really might continue to serve a second 5-year term or even an arbitrary 2-year term. She fears that she could be thrown back in prison at any time, so we continue to pray for Rozita and for so many others as well.

Mr. Chairman, as you know the Iranian regime uses tactics like those that they used against Rozita every day to instill fear in the people of Iran. Iran's human rights practices are amongst the worst in the world. But in its desperation to secure a nuclear deal, the Obama administration has completely ignored the issue of human rights in Iran as well as many other concerns that we have with the Iranian regime.

And this serves as another example of the policy of the White House to look the other way on human rights violations as part of any negotiation, and that was evident in Cuba. The administration is hosting regime officials tomorrow after the Castro state security folks have arrested over 300 civil society activists in the last 3 weeks. In the last 3 weeks. And delegations have come and gone and folks say they are all in favor of human rights, but apparently not while there. Among them was Berta Soler who testified before your subcommittee, Mr. Chairman, 3 weeks ago. In these secret talks with Cuba, the administration showed its willingness to trade away the store for little concessions in return.

So the question becomes what will the administration trade next with the Iran nuclear deal? What will the administration give up in return for those American citizens who are being held in Tehran? The parallels between how the White House is negotiating in secret with Cuba and Iran at the same time—well, the parallels are striking.

What the administration has never understood or really has chosen to ignore is that Congress passed strong sanctions laws not just to stop Iran's nuclear program but also its ballistic missile program, its weapons program, its worldwide support for terror, its destabilization of the region, its abysmal human rights record. And as the author of many pieces of Iran related sanctions legislation, I can tell you that from the beginning the administration fought Congress tooth and nail to stop any sanctions at all.

And so it is of no surprise to anyone that the human rights issue is not even a part of the discussion when we talk about the nuclear deal. And now it appears increasingly likely that the administration will give away what little leverage we have and leave the ayatollahs free to continue to oppress the people of Iran, to continue jailing, torturing, and executing dissidents, prisoners of conscience, religious minorities, and ethnic minorities.

It is truly shameful to hear our own State Department talk about the importance of global human rights, talk about it when it does absolutely nothing and in fact is indirectly legitimizing the continued repression of the people of Iran.

The Obama administration after failing to support the Iranian people's right of self-determination during the 2009 Green Movement rushed to brand Rouhani as a moderate saying that human rights under this Ayatollah lackey would somehow improve.

But what we have seen, Mr. Chairman, is just the opposite. Human rights under Rouhani have actually gotten worse. There have been more crackdowns on free speech, more arrests, more jailings of journalists, more jailings of political prisoners, more persecution of women, the LGBT community, religious minorities, ethnic minorities, more executions.

According to the latest report of Human Rights Watch, the real number of executions in Iran last year is thought to be over 600 including eight who were under the age of 18. We still cannot confirm the execution last week of Saman Naseem, a 22-year-old ethnic Kurd who was 17 when he was arrested. Bloggers and social media users have also suffered under Rouhani with security forces cracking down sharply on any dissent, especially those considered to be leading members of the opposition.

Members of the Baha'i community like Rozita are especially targeted with 100 Baha'is currently in prison. Baha'i cemeteries are systematically destroyed, including last year's bulldozing of over 1,000 graves in one city in order to build a cultural and sports complex. And May 14th is the 7-year anniversary of the imprisonment of the Baha'i Seven, the former leadership group who have been serving 20-year sentences for advocating on behalf of their religious beliefs.

The regime hopes that we will move on, we will forget the people of Iran as the administration in the U.S. continues to negotiate solely on the nuclear program and there are at least four unjustly jailed Americans in Iranian prisons. And we've mentioned them here.

Saeed Abedini, a Christian pastor who has been in jail since 2012 has been tortured and beaten by prison guards and inmates. Marine veteran Amir Hakmati who has been held since 2011. His health is rapidly deteriorating. He is also beaten and tortured. Jason Rezaian, the Washington Post bureau chief arrested last year, still has not been charged but he is in solitary confinement and his health is declining. And of course the constituent of my good friend Ted Deutch, Bob Levinson, a south Florida resident who has been held captive by the Iranian regime since March 9, 2007, making him the longest held hostage in U.S. history. These four U.S. citizens are just a few of the millions who continue to suffer under the Iranian regime, and tragically that suffering is not part of the administration's calculus.

Human rights are an essential factor in long term stability, should be a key objective in our foreign policy strategy, not a simple resolution to pass but something to live up to every day both for those suffering under tyranny and for our own national security.

Mr. Chairman, we must not allow the human rights conditions in Iran to be ignored continually by this administration. Thank you, sir.

Mr. SMITH. Madam Chair, thank you very much for your very eloquent statement and for your passion.

Now we will yield to Mr. Cicilline.

Mr. CICILLINE. Thank you Mr. Chairman, and thank you to you and to Ranking Member Deutch, and thank you to Chairman Ros-Lehtinen for convening this hearing and for calling attention to this very important issue.

While the nuclear negotiations with Iran have dominated discussions in this country of late, the fact remains that Iran remains one of the world's worst perpetrators of human rights abuses and it is critical that we continue to bring attention to this issue. For those who dare to criticize the regime of Supreme Leader Khamenei or attempt to challenge the government and propose conformity, they face harsh consequences sometimes even including death.

I am particularly concerned about the horrific disregard for basic political expression, which according to the current State Department human rights report, they characterize it as the most egregious human rights problems were the government's manipulation of the electoral process, which severely limited citizens' right to change their government peacefully through free and fair elections; restrictions on civil liberties including the freedoms of assembly, speech, and press; and disregard for the physical integrity of persons whom it arbitrarily and unlawfully detained, tortured, and killed. And as was explained, including four American citizens currently being held.

In addition, I am particularly concerned about the rights of LGBT persons and other vulnerable minority groups in the country, in a country that imposes strict, so-called morality codes, does not respect basic freedom of expression or religion and limits access to the outside world.

I thank the witnesses for being here today and look very much forward to your testimony, and again thank the chairman and ranking member for calling this hearing. And with that I yield back.

Mr. SMITH. Thank you.

I would like to yield to Chairman Chabot.

Mr. CHABOT. Thank you, Mr. Chairman. I want to commend you and Chairman Ros-Lehtinen for continuing this series of hearings on Iran, perhaps the most dangerous regime in the world today.

Iran continues to be one of the world's leading abusers of fundamental human rights. The example of the Baha'is which both you and Chairman Ros-Lehtinen talked about already, it has already been referred to, but unfortunately it is only one of many of these abuses which are taking place today.

The regime persecutes anybody who dares to speak publicly or not so publicly against the regime and often issues death sentences to Iranians who are charged with insulting the Islam. It has become pretty clear that the so-called moderate Rouhani is just another in a long list of Iranian dictators whose contempt for his own people's fundamental human rights and religious freedom is readily apparent.

When I chaired the Middle East Subcommittee in not the past, but the one before that Congress, as I had the opportunity to spend about an hour with Prime Minister Netanyahu in his office, and some of the things he told me were shocking and I hadn't heard a lot of them in the news. And one in particular that stands with me to this day was the fact that during the Green Movement they had videos, the government did, and so when they were over we might have thought it was over. And what they were doing is systematically identifying those people that were in the crowds and that were supporters of the Green Movement and they were disappearing and in many instances along with their families, and this was something that got very little attention.

And my colleague, Ms. Ros-Lehtinen, mentioned this administration's, for lack of a better term, dropping the ball, in many instances when it comes to Iran. That was one in particular. I think we had an opportunity to actually speak out and do something on behalf of that movement. That was an opportunity that was missed and a lot of people unfortunately have paid a very high price as a result of that inaction.

And so I want to thank you for holding this hearing and I yield back.

Mr. SMITH. Thank you, Chairman Chabot.

The chair recognizes the gentleman from Michigan, Mr. Trott.

Mr. TROTT. I want to thank Chairman Smith and Chairman Ros-Lehtinen for holding this hearing. And there's no question that

Iran is guilty of egregious human rights violations. They continue to manipulate the election process to prevent peaceful and fair elections. They severely restrict civil liberties, commit repeated religious freedom abuses, show disrespect for the physical integrity of its people through arbitrary detentions and torture and killing.

Other problems include sanctioned amputations and rape and flogging and punishment for politically motivated violence. It is not surprising that the World Press Freedom Index ranked Iran 173rd out of 180 countries with respect to human rights violations.

This hearing is timely for two reasons. First, we have to continue to shine a light and show the terrible abuses that are happening with respect to human rights in Iran, and secondly, Secretary Kerry continues to tell us that we can trust and rely on our negotiations with them and that they need more time. And for me, I submit that a country that is guilty of such egregious abuse cannot be trusted, should not be trusted, and is not worthy of the respect of the world community. Thank you for being here today.

Mr. SMITH. Thank you very much, Mr. Trott.

I would like to now introduce our very distinguished panel beginning first with Shayan Arya who is an expert in Iran, who is also a human rights and political activist. He was elected to the Central Committee of the Constitutionalist Party of Iran in which he served multiple terms. He has co-authored numerous articles focusing on the Iranian regime's human rights violations, internal politics, and terrorist activities. The articles have been published around the world in publications such as the Wall Street Journal, The Australian, the Washington Times, Jerusalem Post, and Strategic Outlook.

We will then hear from Mr. Mohsen Sazegara who was part of the 1979 Islamic Revolution and one of the founders of the Islamic Revolutionary Guards. He held several positions within the regime in the first decade after the revolution, but declined to accept any positions in it after 1988. He has published three newspapers and two monthly magazines which were all shut down by the regime, and has been arrested and imprisoned four times in Iran. While out of the country for medical treatments in 2004, he was sentenced to 6 years of jail. He has continued his political opposition and is currently the president of the Research Institute on Contemporary Iran.

Then we will hear from Mr. Anthony Vance, who oversees the development of the U.S. Baha'i Office of Public Affairs' programs and strategic direction. He joined the office in 2010 after spending 4 years at the Baha'i World Center in Haifa, Israel, representing it to the diplomatic community, civil society, and to the host government. A lawyer by training, he spent 21 years in the U.S. Agency for International Development in legal and managerial positions in Washington, Cote d'Ivoire, Kenya, Botswana, and Egypt.

Mr. Arya, if you could begin.

STATEMENT OF MR. SHAYAN ARYA, CENTRAL COMMITTEE MEMBER, CONSTITUTIONALIST PARTY OF IRAN (LIBERAL DEMOCRAT)

Mr. ARYA. Chairman Smith, Chairman Ros-Lehtinen, and honorable members of the subcommittees, it is really an honor to appear before you today to discuss the human rights situation in Iran under the Islamic regime. It is an important issue that has unfortunately been overlooked by the international community in light of the current negotiations between Iran and P5+1 since the election of Hassan Rouhani as President of Iran in 2013.

Since that time, the Iranian regime, its supporters and lobbyists have tried vigorously to convince the international community in general and the U.S. administration in particular that something has fundamentally changed for the better in Iran, that the Iran Islamic Republic can be trusted to act according to Iran's national interests and not its ideological ones. Unfortunately however the regime's actions speak louder than its words.

Iran, after China, currently has the highest number of executions in the world, and since Rouhani's election there has not been a reduction in that statistic. To the contrary, there has been a significant increase. In 2014 alone, eight individuals believed to be under 18 years of age at the time of their alleged crimes were reportedly executed. Human rights activists in Iran put the total number of executions for 2013 and 2014 at 1,181 people.

The execution of juveniles is not the only crime committed by the Islamic Republic. The Islamic regime systematically tries to brainwash children. On this important issue I would like to draw your attention to the research done by the Institute for Monitoring Peace and Cultural Tolerance in School Education, IMPACT-se. The Islamic Republic systematically indoctrinates children and prepares them for war and encourage the hostile attitude toward non-Muslims with children instructed not to take unbelievers, Jews and Christians as friends.

Again, against this background is it any surprise that almost all religious minorities in Iran suffer officially sanctioned discriminations? Baha'is are banned from all government positions, are not allowed to have places of worship, and are banned from teaching the faith and even attend universities. In some cases they have even been denied burial sites and their cemeteries are systematically destroyed.

Evangelical Christians are suffering as well. Even Muslims who do not conform to the official interpretation of Islam face heresy charges. Last September, Mohsen Amir-Aslani was executed for insulting the prophet Jonah by declaring that his story in Koran was symbolic rather than factual.

Even traditional Shiite clerics who reject official interpretation of Islam are persecuted. Ayatollah Hossein Kazemeyni Boroujerdi is a traditional Shiite cleric who openly questions the legitimacy of the Islamic Republic and advocates a secular regime and has been imprisoned since 2007. Followers of Ahl-e Haqq religion are also under enormous pressure. Several members of the Ahl-e Haqq community have self-immolated in recent years to protest against religious persecution in Iran.

The Nematollahi-Gonabadi Sufi order is another example. Many members of this Sufi order are presently imprisoned and several places of their worship in Isfahan and other cities have been demolished. Mohammad Ali Taheri, founder of a spiritual group, was also arrested in 2011. In fact yesterday some of his supporters came out in support of him and many of them were arrested, just yesterday.

Iran is one of the few countries in the world that prosecutes lawyers for representing their clients. Ms. Nasrin Sotudeh and Abdolfattah Soltani are good examples. Mr. Soltani, a leading human rights lawyer has even been denied medical attention despite the fact that even prison doctors have written a letter recommending that he be treated outside the prison.

Last March, Maryam Shafipour, 29 years old, was sentenced to 7 years in prison for peaceful protests. Many student activists such as Majid Tavakkoli, Bhareh Hedayat, Sayed Zia Nabavi, Majid Dori, and Navid Khanjani have spent years, years in prisons for no crimes other than exercising their rights to peaceful protest.

A young brilliant scientist, Mr. Omid Kokabee, has been incarcerated in Evin prison since 2011. He was charged with espionage and for refusing not to work on military research projects with the government. That was his only crime.

Atena Farghadani, a children's rights advocate currently is in prison and she is on hunger strike. And what she's asking, not be released but to be moved from Gharchak prison which is a notoriously substandard women prison, to be moved back to Evin prison. And she's in a very dire situation right now from what I heard yesterday.

Political activists such as Heshmatollah Tabarzadi have spent years in prison for their peaceful activities. Just a few days ago, Masood Arab Choobdar, Saeed Shirzad, Hamid Babaei who were exiled from Tehran to Rajaei Shahr prison, which is another notoriously dangerous prison in Iran, they were beaten and severely abused. Another Baha'i prisoner, Shahram Chinian was also beaten, so severely that his face was unrecognizable by his friends.

Last July, Iranian writer Arzhang Davoodi was sentenced to death after spending nearly 11 years in prison on new charges of enmity against God in relation to his political activism and writings in support of a secular system. Journalists are another group that suffer under the Islamic Republic. According to Committee to Protect Journalists currently there are 30 journalists in Iran in prison.

These cases are simply a reflection of the Iranian regime's repressive domestic practices. The main question then is whether these practices are changing and whether Iran's new President Hassan Rouhani is really a reformer. To understand Mr. Rouhani's relationship to the state it is necessary to review his background. He has been a member of Islamic regime's leadership for the past 36 years and therefore has been an integral part of every aggressive move that the Islamic Republic has made since 1982. From creation and training of Hezbollah to the 1983 attack on U.S. and French military forces in Lebanon, the assassination of nearly 200 Iranian dissidents in Europe throughout the 1980s and 1990s, the 1994 bombing in Buenos Aires, and more recently to the Iranian's asymmetric campaign targeting U.S. and coalition forces in Iraq.

It is impossible to believe that Mr. Rouhani had no knowledge of these actions. Rouhani's cabinet choice for the post of Justice Minister, Mostafa Pourmohammadi, speaks volumes to his commitment to the issue of human rights. Pourmohammadi had direct role in the extrajudicial executions of thousands of political prisoners in the 1980s.

As we all know, Iran is the only country in the Middle East where people are by and large are friendly to America, therefore it is crucial that America stands up to the Islamic Republic on this important issue. I would like to encourage the honorable members of the subcommittees on behalf of all those who are suffering in the hands of the Islamic regime to link any easing or lifting of sanctions not just to the outcome of the nuclear negotiations but also to the improvement in the human rights situation in Iran.

With that I would like to thank you again for this opportunity and would be more than happy to answer any questions.

[The prepared statement of Mr. Arya follows:]

"The Shame of Iranian Human Rights"

February 26, 2015

Statement before the

U.S. House of Representative Committee on Foreign Affairs

Edward R. Royce (R-CA), Chairman

Subcommittee on Africa, Global Health, Global Human Rights and International Organization

Christopher H. Smith (R-NJ), Chairman

Subcommittee on the Middle East and North Africa

Ileana Ros-Lethinen (R-FL), Chairman

Shayan Arya

Central Committee

The Constitutionalist Party of Iran (Liberal Democrat)

Chairman Royce, Chairman Smith, Chairman Ros-Lethinen, honorable members of the Subcommittees:

It is truly an honor to appear before you today to discuss the human rights situation in Iran under the Islamic regime and the nature of the terrorist regime in Iran. It is an important issue that has unfortunately been overlooked by the international community in light of current negotiations between Iran and the P5+1 since the election of Hassan Rouhani as president of Iran in 2013.

Since that time, the Iranian regime, its supporters and lobbyists have tried vigorously to convince the international community in general and the U.S. administration in particular that something has fundamentally changed for the better in Iran. Rouhani's administration, they argue, is a moderate one, and one that will make the Islamic Republic into a more open, transparent and above all, a normal regime which can be trusted.. Unfortunately, however, the regime's actions speak louder than its words.

Following China, Iran currently has the highest number of executions in the world[1], and since Rouhani's election there has not been a reduction in these statistics. To the contrary, there has been a significant increase. As the most recent report of United Nations Special Rapporteur Ahmad Shaheed notes, "Between July 2013 and June 2014, at least 852 individuals were reportedly executed, representing an alarming increase in the number of executions in relation to the already-high rates of previous years." According to the report, the Iranian government "also continues to execute juvenile offenders. In 2014 alone, eight individuals believed to be under 18 years of age at the time of their alleged crimes were reportedly executed."[2] Human Rights activists in Iran put the total number of executions for 2013 and 2014 at 1181 people.[3]

The execution of juveniles is not the only crime committed by the Islamic Republic. The Iranian regime systematically tries to brainwash it's children. In 2007, the Institute for Monitoring Peace and Cultural Tolerance in School Education, IMPACT-se, a remarkable research institute that I have had the honor of cooperating with briefly, published a detailed and thorough study of Iranian school curriculums. It concluded that the Islamic Republic uses schoolbooks to systematically indoctrinate children and to prepare them for war against America and other "non-believers." It furthermore found that Iran's school curriculum systematically encourages a hostile attitude towards non-Muslims, with children instructed to not to take "unbelievers"," Jews" and "Christians" as friends.[4]

Not surprisingly, the books have not changed much. Here is a quote from an 8th grade book, the form the upcoming IMPAC-SE 2015 report that covered the Iranian curriculum of 2012 – 2014: "Jihad means effort and combat (*talash va mobarezeh*) in God's way and defense of Muslims and oppressed (*mazluman*) in order to maintain the right and the true (*haqq va haqiqat*), unity and justice, to eliminate transgression and plunder (*tajavoz va chapavol*), torture and intimidation, occupation and colonialism, and in general, sedition and corruption in the world.[5]

Iranian text books proudly admit that "During the eight years of Holy Defense [that is, the war with Iraq] more than 500,000 school students were sent to the fronts. 36,000 martyrs, thousands of missing-in-action, invalids, and liberated [prisoners-of-war] of this sacrificing section were offered to the Islamic Revolution".[6] This is the role model Iranian children are to emulate - and Iranian children are thus brainwashed to follow their examples.

Islamic Republic violates the United Nations Convention on The Rights of the Child which states, "The child shall have the right to freedom of expression; this right shall include freedom

---

[1] http://www.theguardian.com/news/datablog/2011/mar/29/death-penalty-countries-world

[2] http://shaheedoniran.org/wp-content/uploads/2014/09/A-69-356-SR-Report-Iran.pdf
[3] https://hra-news.org/fa/wp-content/uploads/2015/01/hra-annual-report-2014-farsi.pdf
[4] http://www.impact-se.org/research/iran/index.html

[5] Ahkam (Religious Rulings): Acquaintance with the Rulings, Grade 8, 1391, P.12
[6] Defense Readiness, Grade 11 (2012-3), p. 11

to seek, receive and impart information and ideas of all kinds, regardless of frontiers, either orally, in writing or in print, in the form of art, or through any other media of the child's choice. United Nations Convention on the Rights of the Child (article 13)."[7]

Iran is demographically a very young country. Approximately 70 to 75 percent of Iran's population is under the age of 40. This means that nearly 60 million Iranians have gone through Iran's educational system and have been exposed to this systematic brainwashing. Fortunately, it can be said that this effort has failed; the overwhelming majority of Iranian youth are anti-regime and have a positive views of America. However, the Islamic Republic does not need to be 100% successful to pose a grave danger. Even a very small percentage of school age children successfully indoctrinated translate into tens or even hundreds of thousands of radicals who are brainwashed to view America and adherents of religions other than Islam as enemies.

Despite his moderate posture and diplomatic language, Mr. Rouhani is part of the problem. As a member of Iran's National Security Council, not only is he aware of the contents of Iran's curriculum; he helped to approve them. Against this background, is it any surprise that almost all religious minority in Iran: Baha'is, Christians, Sufi's or Dervish Muslims, Sunnis and Ahle-Hagh suffer officially sanctioned discrimination?

Baha'is, one of the largest non-Muslim religious minorities, are considered by the Islamic Republic not as a religious minority but as a "subversive sect," or "Fergheh-e-zalleh." As such, they are subject to widespread discrimination. Baha'is are banned from all government positions. They are not allowed to have places of worship and are banned from teaching the faith. Young members of the Bahai faith are barred from universities and higher education.

The "Universal Declaration of Human Rights" states clearly that "Everyone has the right to education." Yet the Iranian regime systematically seeks to deprive Bahais of this right. Any student who is found to be Baha'I is immediately expelled.

For example, Paniz Fazl-Ali, a talented civil engineering student at Iran's University of Science and Technology (IUST) in Tehran, was expelled for no other reason than adhering to the Baha'i faith.[8] Baha'i World News Services also reports that Islamic regime has also "sought to close down Baha'i efforts to establish their own educational initiatives, including the Baha'i Institute for Higher education".[9]

Anyone involved with educating Baha'is will also be arrested. Ahmad Shaheed's report to the UN indicates that "at least 126 Baha'is were held in detention as of August 2014".[10] The Islamic

---

[7] http://www.impact-se.org/docs/articles/State_Sponsored_Child_Abuse_in_Iran%207.11.07.pdf

[8] http://www.theguardian.com/world/2013/feb/27/bahai-student-expelled-iranian-university

[9] http://news.bahai.org/human-rights/iran/education/

[10] http://shaheedoniran.org/wp-content/uploads/2014/09/A-69-356-SR-Report-Iran.pdf

Republic also systematically destroys Baha'i cemeteries. As recently as May 2014, officials from the Islamic Revolutionary Guard Corps demolished a Baha'i cemetery in Shiraz. [11]

In some cases, Bahai's are even denied burial sites. Last November we heard about a twelve-year-old, Mahna Samandari who passed away and for weeks her parents were not able to bury her because the local authorities denied them the right to bury their child in the local cemetery of Tabriz.

In another case Narges Khatounbargi, an 85-year old Bahai woman was barred from being buried in the general cemetery in Tabriz as well. Both Mahna and Narges had to be taken to another town, Miandoab, for burial. [12] Islamic regime's pressure on Baha'is has intensified and several Baha'i families have been forced to sell their shops. [13] The pattern is clear; Iranian authorities are systematically trying to close all doors to Baha'is so they will have no choice but to leave Iran.

Evangelical Christians are also under enormous pressure. Iranian-American Pastor Saeed Abedini has been imprisoned since 2012. Mr. Abedini was arrested and charged with "enmity against God", "spreading corruption on earth" and "actions against national security". He was tortured and sentenced to eight years in prison. [14]

Islamic Republic considers converts to Christianity as apostates and apostasy under Islamic penal code is punishable by death. Although the number of Christian converts executed by the Iranian regime is not as high as those of the Baha'i faith, it nevertheless underscores that Iranians are not free to choose their own religion- a state of affairs that is contrary to article 18 of the "Universal Declaration of Human Rights," which states: "Everyone has the right to freedom of thought, conscience and religion; this right includes freedom to change his religion or belief, and freedom, either alone or in community with others and in public or private, to manifest his religion or belief in teaching, practice, worship and observance." [15]

Baha'is and Christians are not the only groups who face apostasy charges under the Islamic Republic's penal code. Even Muslims who do not conform to the official interpretation of Islam face heresy charges.

Last September, a 37-year-old man, Mr. Mohsen Amir-Aslani, was executed for insulting the Prophet Jonah by declaring that his story in the Quran was symbolic rather than factual. [16] His case is important since up until few weeks prior to his execution; his family had refrained from publicizing his case in hopes of his release. They apparently could not believe that he will be executed for such a ridiculous charge.

---

[11] http://news.bahai.org/story/993

[12] https://hra-news.org/en/tag/mahna-samandari

[13] http://news.bahai.org/story/1027

[14] http://www.christianitytoday.com/gleanings/2015/january/obama-to-imprisoned-pastors-wife-save-saeed-abedini-naghmeh.html?paging=off

[15] http://www.un.org/en/documents/udhr/index.shtml#a18

[16] http://www.theguardian.com/world/2014/sep/29/iran-executes-man-heresy-mohsen-amir-aslani

Even traditional Shiite clerics who reject the official interpretation of Islam are persecuted. Ayatollah Hossein Kazemeini Boroujerdi, a traditional Shiite cleric who openly and unapologetically questions the legitimacy of the Islamic Republic and advocates a secular regime with a total separation of religion from the government has been imprisoned since 2007. He has been tortured repeatedly with his properties confiscated. He has not changed his views despite the enormous pressure exerted on him and his family by the regime.[17]

Followers of Ahle-Hagh religion, a peaceful, ancient non-Muslim minority who live primarily in Kurdish province are also under enormous pressure and are subject to systematic discrimination. Several members of the Ahle- Hagh community have self-immolated in recent years to protest religious persecution in Iran.[18]

Another group under pressure with their rights denied are the Nematollahi Gonabadi Suifs: a peaceful religious order with deep roots in Iran. Many members of this Sufi order are presently imprisoned and several places of their worships in Isfahan and other cities have been demolished by the Iranian authorities.[19] [20]

Muhammad Ali Taheri, founder of a spiritual group with different interpretation of Islam, was arrested in May 2011. He has been kept in solitary confinement and will go on trial this year. In Nov 2014, he embarked on a hunger strike for 25 days to protest 3.5 years of solitary confinement. [21]Political activists, student activists, human rights activists, worker's right activists, and even lawyers who represent dissidents suffer as well.

The Islamic Republic of Iran is of the few countries in the world that prosecutes lawyers for representing their clients. Ms. Nassrin Sotudeh, a human rights lawyer who represented imprisoned Iranian opposition activists and politicians after the 2009 uprising was arrested in 2010 on charges of spreading propaganda and conspiring to harm state security. She spent months in solitary confinement. She was recently released but has a three-year ban from practicing law.

In another case, imprisoned Iranian lawyer Abdolfattah Soltani, a leading human rights lawyer has even been denied medical attention despite a letter written by prison doctors recommending that he be treated outside the prison.[22] He will go on trial on "corruption on earth" charges.[23]

---

[17] http://www.weeklystandard.com/blogs/jailed-iranian-ayatollah-calls-regime-worse-and-more-evil-isis-or-taliban_818523.html

[18] http://blog.iranrights.org/third-dervish-self-immolates-to-protest-religious-persecution-in-iran/

[19] http://www.europarl.europa.eu/meetdocs/2009_2014/documents/d-ir/dv/hr_violations_dervish/hr_violations_dervishes.pdf

[20] http://www.huffingtonpost.com/stephen-schwartz/iran-continues-crackdown-on-sufis_b_3181642.html

[21] http://www.iranhumanrights.org/2015/02/mohammad-ali-taheri-2/

[22] http://www.iranhumanrights.org/2014/12/abdolfattah-soltani/

[23] http://www.iranhumanrights.org/2015/02/mohammad-ali-taheri-2/

Students are not in better shape.

Last March, Maryam Shafipour, 29, was sentenced to seven years in prison for participating in a peaceful protest. [24] Many student activists such as Majid Tavakkoli,[25] Bahareh Hedayat,[26] Seyed Zia Nabavi, [27]Majid Dori[28] and Navid Khanjani [29]have spent years in prison for no crime other than exercising their right to peaceful protest.

The 32-year-old brilliant physicist, Mr. Omid Kokabee, has been incarcerated in Evin prison since January 2011. He was charged with espionage for refusing to work on military research projects. He was awarded the American Association for the Advancement of Science (AAAS) in 2014.[30] 31 Nobel Physics laureates signed a petition, and called for his release.[31] He is still in jail.

Not only student activists, but children rights and civil rights activists are also under pressure. Atena Farghadani, a children's right and civil rights activist was arrested[32]. She was later moved to Gharchak prison, a notoriously substandard women's prison. She is currently on a hunger strike

Political activists such as Heshmatollah Tabarzadi have spent years in prison for their peaceful activities. Just a few days ago, Masoud Arab Chubdar, Saeed Shirzad, Hamid Babaei, a PhD student from Belgium who refused to spy for the regime and was sentenced to six years in prison,[33] were exiled from Evin prison to the Rajaei Shahr Prison, a notoriously unsafe prison in Karaj. Another Baha'i Prisoner Shahram Chinian was beaten so severely that his face was unrecognizable by his friends. Arash Moghadam was also severely beaten.

Last July Amnesty International reported that Iranian writer Arzhang Davoodi was sentenced to death after spending nearly 11 years in prison on new charges of "enmity against God" in relation to his peaceful political activism and writings in support of secularism.[34]

Journalists are another group that suffers under the Islamic Republic. According to "Committee to Protect Journalists" currently there are 30 Journalists in Iranian prisons. [35]

---

[24] http://www.theguardian.com/world/iran-blog/2014/mar/03/iran-sentences-student-activist-seven-years-prison-maryam-shafipour

[25] http://www.theguardian.com/world/2013/oct/22/politicial-prisoner-majid-tavakoli-bail

[26] https://tavaana.org/en/content/bahareh-hedayat-womens-rights-defender

[27] http://iran.usembassy.gov/zianabavi.html

[28] http://iran.usembassy.gov/dorimajid.html

[29] https://tavaana.org/en/content/iran-violation-rights-education-navid-khanjani%E2%80%99s-testimony

[30] http://www.iranhumanrights.org/2015/02/omid-kokabee-3/

[31] http://www.iranhumanrights.org/2014/10/31-nobel-laureates/

[32] https://hra-news.org/en/atena-faraghdani-childrens-rights-activist-arrested

[33] http://www.iranhrc.org/?p=968

[34] Iranian prisoner of conscience Arzhang Davoodi, already in prison for nearly 11 years, has now been sentenced to death on a new charge of "enmity against God", in relation to his peaceful political activism and writings.

Unfortunately, there is nothing unique or new about the above mentioned cases. They are simply a reflection of the Iranian regime's repressive domestic practices. The main question, then, is whether those practices are changing – and whether Iran's new president, Hassan Rouhani, can be considered a reformer?

To understand Mr. Rouhani's relationship to the state, it is necessary to review his background. Iran's new president has been a member of Islamic regime's leadership for the past 36 years. He was the head of the executive committee of the country's Defense Council from 1982 to 1988. The end of the Iran-Iraq war in 1988 was followed by the creation of the Supreme National Security Council, and since that time Rouhani has been the representative of the Supreme Leader, Ayatollah Khamenei, in that forum. From 1991 until now, he has also been a member of the Expediency Council, the most powerful governing body in Iran charged with mediating disputes between the parliament and the Guardian Council, [36] where he heads its Political, Defense, and Security Committee.

These dates are important, since they make clear that Mr. Rouhani has been an integral part of every aggressive move the Islamic Republic has made since 1982.

These include the1982 decision to continue the conflict with Iraq for another six years at the cost of hundreds of thousands of Iranian lives; the establishment of a base in the Syrian controlled Bekaa Valley the same year, and the subsequent creation and training of proxy terror group Hezbollah; the 1983 attacks on U.S. and French military forces in Lebanon; the assassination of nearly 200 Iranian dissidents and prominent opposition leaders during the 1980s and 1990s, The 1994 AMIA bombing in Buenos Aires, and more recently, the Iranian asymmetric campaigns targeting U.S. and Coalition soldiers in both Afghanistan and Iraq.

Is it possible to believe that Mr. Rouhani, who has served in the upper echelons of the Islamic Republic for all these years, had no knowledge of these actions? Are these the "reform" that emerges under his watch? ? Is it possible to think of him as a peacemaker? Is it possible to think of him as a person who cares about human rights in Iran? And above all, is it possible to trust him on these issues? Rouhani's cabinet choice for the post of Justice Minister, Mostafa Pour-Muhammadi, may give an indication on his judgment.

Pour-Muhammadi is indeed a pursuer of "Justice." "Human Rights Watch, in a 2005 report titled "Ministers of Murder," [37] documented Pour-Mohammadi's direct role in the extrajudicial executions of thousands of political prisoners."[38]

For me, a member of Iran's democratic opposition, the answer to these questions and many others is a resounding "NO".

---

[35] https://www.cpj.org/imprisoned/2014.php#iran

[36] http://www.pbs.org/wgbh/pages/frontline/shows/tehran/inside/govt.html

[37] http://www.hrw.org/legacy/backgrounder/mena/iran1205/iran1205.pdf

[38] http://www.hrw.org/news/2013/08/08/iran-withdraw-cabinet-nominee-implicated-abuses

Mr. SMITH. Thank you very much for your testimony, and without objection your full statement will be made a part of the record as well as our other distinguished witnesses.

Mr. Sazegara, please proceed.

STATEMENT OF MR. MOHSEN SAZEGARA, PRESIDENT, RESEARCH INSTITUTE ON CONTEMPORARY IRAN

Mr. SAZEGARA. Thank you, Mr. Chairman. Thank you, subcommittee members.

During the last three and a half decades, the Iranian people have bitterly experienced suppression of their fundamental freedoms and rights and witnessed brutal crackdowns of pro-freedom movements in Iran. I deeply regret to say that extensive and systematic violations of human rights, persecutions, unfair trials, unfounded imprisonments, tortures, rapes, and extrajudicial executions still continue despite the pledges Mr. Rouhani had made to change this trend during his election campaign in 2013.

Regardless of some rare cosmetic and non-systemic release of a dozen of well-known prisoners in 2013 and 2014, the human rights abuses have not only continued but also increased in many respects, including but not limited to imprisonment of human rights activists, journalists, bloggers, university students and teachers, workers, ethnic and religious minorities, and political opposition.

In 2014, the cases of arrest, detention, and imprisonment of activists illustrate a 74-percent increase as compared to 2013. This average increase comprises 53 percent increase in ethnic minorities cases, 10 percent in religious, 93 percent students, 410 percent freedom of expression and conscience, and 354 percent in labor activists cases.

Another human rights violation in Iran includes persistent and pervasive assault on women on a continued basis under the pretext of disrespecting hijab, education and employment segregation, and being banned from appearing on stage for musical performances.

Torture of political prisoners continues to coerce fabricated confessions that are then used to justify brutal crackdowns. According to first hand reports received from former political prisoners, the main methods of torture include whipping and assault, sexual torture including rape, and psychological torture such as prolonged solitary confinement. These reports are also in conformity with the reports by Dr. Shaheed, the U.N. Special Rapporteur on the Situation of Human Rights in Iran.

Execution in Iran has increased from 544 known cases in 2012 to more than 800 known cases in 2014, it being the highest per capita rate in the world. The numbers are however suspected to be higher since many of these executions are carried out in secret and the regime has consistently refrained from releasing numbers and denied the U.N. Special Rapporteur's access to the country.

These are only examples of a range of human rights violation categories. Such extensive and systematic violations of human rights should not come as a surprise. Despite talk of moderation, Rouhani has indulged impunity and rewarded the perpetrators of such grave abuses. His present Justice Minister Mr. Pourmohammadi who played, as a member of the notorious ''death committee,'' a key role in the 1988 prison massacre, has been appointed by this very ''moderate'' government.

In the end, I cordially submit that a standing subcommittee be formed under the Subcommittee on the Middle East and North Africa in order to monitor and take all the necessary measures to draw the world's attention to the grave human rights abuses in Iran. Enclosed I have submitted the first two proposals to be put on the docket of this subcommittee. Thank you very much.

[The prepared statement of Mr. Sazegara follows:]

Extensive and systematic Human Rights violation in Iran continues!
Presented by: Mohsen Sazegara, President of Research Institute on Contemporary Iran

Ladies and Gentlemen!

During the last three and a half decades, the Iranian people have bitterly experienced suppression of their fundamental freedoms and rights, and witnessed brutal crackdowns of pro-freedom movements in Iran. I deeply regret to say that extensive and systematic violations of human rights, persecutions, unfair trials, unfounded imprisonments, tortures, rapes and extrajudicial executions still continue, despite the pledges Mr. Rouhani had made to change this trend during his election campaign in 2013.

Regardless of some rare cosmetic and non-systemic release of a dozen of well-known prisoners in 2013 and 2014, the human rights abuses have not only continued, but also increased in many respects including, but not limited to, imprisonment of human rights activists, journalists, bloggers, university students and teachers, workers, ethnic and religious minorities, and political opposition. In 2014, the cases of arrest, detention and imprisonment of activists illustrate a 74 percent increase as compared to 2013. This average increase comprises 53 percent increase in ethnic minorities cases, 10 percent in religious, 93 percent students, 410 percent freedom of expression and conscience, and 354 percent in labor activists cases.

Another human rights violation in Iran includes, *inter alia*, persistent and pervasive assault on women on a continued basis on the pretext of disrespecting Hejab, education and employment segregation, and being banned from appearing on stage for musical performances.

Torture of political prisoners continues to coerce fabricated confessions that are then used to justify brutal crackdowns. According to first-hand reports received from former political prisoners, the main methods of torture include whipping and assault; sexual torture including rape; and psychological torture such as prolonged solitary confinement. These reports are also in conformity with the reports by Dr. Shahid, the UN Special Rapporteur on the Situation of Human Rights in Iran.

Execution in Iran has increased from 544 known cases in 2012, to more than 800 known cases in 2014, it being the highest per capita rate in the world. The numbers are, however, suspected to be higher since many of these executions are carried out in secret, and the regime has consistently refrained from releasing numbers, and denied the UN Special Rapporteur's access to the country.

These are only examples of a range of human rights violations categories. Such extensive and systematic violations of human rights should not come as a surprise. Despite talk of moderation, Rouhani has indulged impunity, and rewarded the perpetrators of such grave abuses. His present Justice Minister one Pour-Mohammadi who played, as a member of the notorious Death Committee, a key role in the 1988 Prison Massacre, has been appointed by this very "moderate" government.

In the end, I cordially submit that a Standing Subcommittee be formed under the Subcommittee on the Middle East and North Africa in order to monitor and take all the necessary measures to draw the world's attention to the grave human rights abuses in Iran. Enclosed, I have submitted the first two proposals to be put on the docket of this Subcommittee.

Thank you very much!

**Human Rights Abuse Reports Categories in Iran Based
(2013 and 2014)**

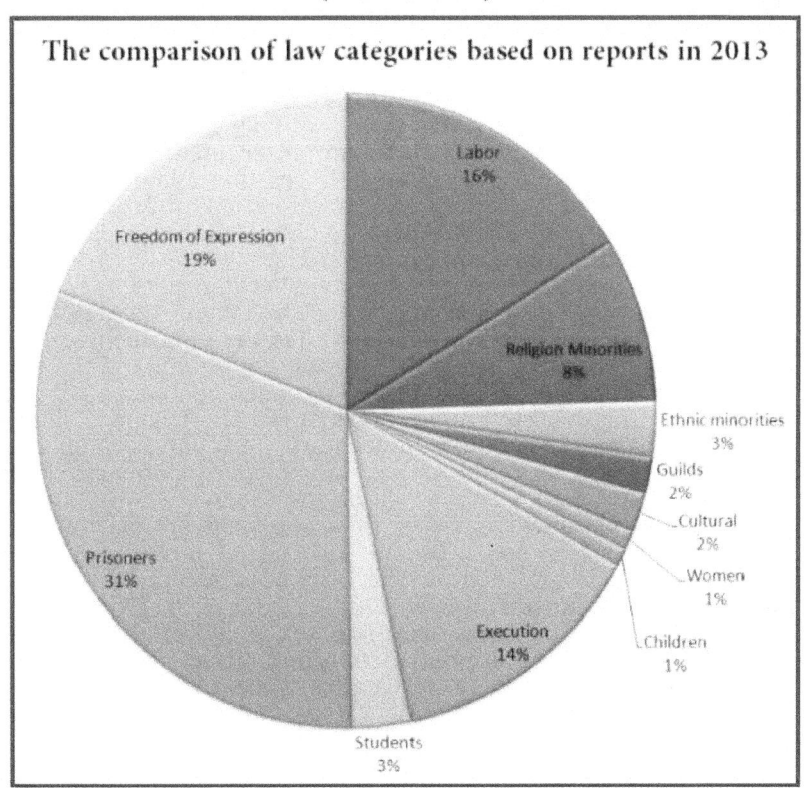

NB: In 2014, the most significant changes in the abuse reports were in reports about Prisoners (23% increased to 31%), Women (1% to 5%), Religious Minorities (8% to 12%) and Children (1% to 4%). *Source: Human Rights Activists In Iran (HRA)*

Mr. SMITH. Thank you very much.

Yes, thank you so much for that testimony. Both of you brought up the fact that the Justice Minister is in this "moderate" government serving in a high position despite his horrific past.

I would like to now ask Mr. Vance if you would proceed.

STATEMENT OF MR. ANTHONY VANCE, DIRECTOR, U.S. BAHA'I OFFICE OF PUBLIC AFFAIRS

Mr. VANCE. Chairman Smith, Chairman Ros-Lehtinen and also Chairman Chabot, I would like to thank you for giving me the opportunity to testify on the situation of the Baha'is of Iran.

A little background, I think, is appropriate. The Baha'i Faith is an independent world religion with over 5 million followers in over 200 countries and territories representing virtually every racial, ethnic, and national group on the planet.

The faith originated in Iran. It spread rapidly in the mid-1840s immediately after its inception and included several notable clerics among its initial adherents. This triggered a violent reaction instigated or supported by a majority of the clergy, during which some 20,000 Baha'is were killed over little more than a decade.

The primary reason that Baha'is are persecuted is theological. Most of the Islamic clergy in Iran believes that Islam is the final religion of God. The Baha'i Faith, a religion that arose after Islam, is therefore viewed by most of Iran's clergy as heresy and blasphemy, and Baha'is are viewed as apostates.

In addition, Iran's clerics view certain teachings of the Baha'i Faith as threatening. For instance, the Baha'i Faith does not have a clergy and holds that each individual has the duty to investigate spiritual truth and arrive at his or her own beliefs. In addition, Baha'is believe strongly in the equality of women and men.

Now while the intense brutality against Baha'is began to subside toward the end of the nineteenth century, unequal treatment, social hostilities and sporadic surges in violence continued during much of the twentieth century. After the Islamic Revolution of 1979, Baha'is became the target of severe and systematic state-sponsored persecution and it became official government policy to oppress Baha'is.

In the years following the revolution, over 200 Baha'is were killed, the majority by execution. Thousands of Baha'is were imprisoned, many of them tortured. Baha'i holy places were destroyed and Baha'i cemeteries have repeatedly been attacked and desecrated, including the current ongoing excavation of the large Baha'i cemetery in Shiraz.

The government also made and continues to make concerted efforts to impoverish the Baha'i community. After the revolution, Baha'is were dismissed from government jobs and denied pensions and private employers have been pressured not to hire Baha'is. Baha'is still suffer frequent raids on their homes and businesses, including a recent spate of shop closures, and their property is routinely seized without compensation.

Baha'is were also dismissed from university positions after the revolution, and Baha'i students have been excluded from the nation's universities and continue to be so. The seven members of the former ad hoc leadership group of the Baha'i community are among the 100 Baha'is currently imprisoned in Iran, nearly twice the number that were imprisoned at the end of 2010.

In the last several months there has also been a disturbing surge in anti-Baha'i hate propaganda in state-sponsored media outlets. In 2010 and 2011, approximately 22 anti-Baha'i pieces were appearing every month. In 2014, the number of anti-Baha'i pieces rose to approximately 401 per month, 18 times the previous level.

In July 2013, the Supreme Leader Ali Khamenei reissued a religious decree prohibiting Iranian Muslims from associating with members of the ''deviant sect,'' a well-known reference to Baha'is. The clerical establishment has long promoted the view that Baha'is are ritually unclean and that the blood of Baha'is is mobah, meaning that it can be spilled with impunity.

Last October, the review of Iran's human rights record before the U.N. Human Rights Council revealed that Iran had failed to live up to dozens of promises made during its last Universal Periodic Review in 2010, including several related to the Baha'is. Yet in an astonishingly blatant falsehood, Iran's written response to the council declared ''minorities, including Baha'is, enjoyed a full range of opportunities and privileges.''

It is our hope that at the follow-up session on Iran that will be held next month, responsible nations will emphasize the persecution of the Baha'is and countless other individuals and will hold the Iranian Government to account for its gross violations of human rights. Thank you very much, Mr. Chairman.

[The prepared statement of Mr. Vance follows:]

BAHÁ'ÍS OF THE UNITED STATES

Testimony of
Anthony N. Vance
Director of Public Affairs
Bahá'ís of the United States

Thursday, February 26, 2015

Hearing: "The Shame of Iranian Human Rights"

United States House of Representatives
Committee on Foreign Affairs
Subcommittee on Africa, Global Health, Global Human Rights and International Organizations
Subcommittee on the Middle East and North Africa

Chairman Smith, Ranking Member Bass, Chairman Ros-Lehtinen, Ranking Member Deutch and Members of the Subcommittee, I would like to thank you for giving me the opportunity to testify on the situation of the Bahá'í's in Iran. I would like to request that my written statement be included in the record.

I am the Director of Public Affairs for the Bahá'ís of the United States. The Bahá'í Faith is an independent world religion with over five million followers in over 200 countries and territories, representing virtually every racial, ethnic, and national group on the planet.

The Bahá'í Faith originated in Persia, modern-day Iran, and Bahá'ís in that country have been persecuted since the inception of the Faith in the mid-nineteenth century. With roughly 300,000 members, the Bahá'í community in Iran is the largest non-Muslim religious minority in the country. The UN Special Rapporteur on freedom of religion or belief, Heiner Bielefeldt, has stated that the plight of the Bahá'ís in Iran is one of the clearest cases of state-sponsored persecution.

The primary reason that Bahá'ís are persecuted is theological. The Islamic clergy in Iran subscribes to an orthodox view that Islam is the final religion of God and that there can be no religion after it. The Bahá'í Faith, a religion that arose after Islam, is therefore viewed by most of Iran's clergy as heresy and blasphemy, and Bahá'ís are viewed as apostates.

In the early years after the founding of the Faith, the religion spread quickly, gaining many adherents among all classes of society, including respected and powerful Muslim clergymen. The clerical establishment thus perceived the movement as a threat and reacted violently to it, exerting its influence to suppress or eliminate early Bahá'í communities. In the first two decades of the Faith, some 20,000 Bahá'ís were killed by the forces of the Shah and by mobs, instigated by members of the clergy. The authorities also carried out massacres and public executions, as well as widespread imprisonment and torture.

Bahá'ís have also been persecuted for social reasons. Certain teachings of the Bahá'í Faith are viewed as threatening by the clerical establishment in Iran. For instance, the Bahá'í Faith does not have a clergy and holds that each individual has the duty to investigate spiritual truth and arrive at his her own beliefs. In addition, Baha'is believe strongly in the equality of women and men.

Finally, Bahá'ís have, in some sense, been targeted simply for being a minority. The treatment of Bahá'ís in Iran is a prime example of scapegoating, a phenomenon that has occurred in many societies throughout history, in which ethnic or religious minorities are targeted in times of societal difficulties and are irrationally and unfairly blamed for all manner of political, economic, and social problems.

While the intense brutality against Bahá'ís began to subside toward the end of the nineteenth century, unequal treatment continued. During much of the twentieth century, when Iran witnessed a fairly rapid period of development, the pressure on the Bahá'is lessened. However, Bahá'is still faced discrimination and were often denied opportunities. They were also subject to social hostilities, such as interpersonal violence, acts of arson, and the desecration of cemeteries, which usually went unaddressed by authorities. For instance, in one notable incident in 1955, a prominent cleric, with the knowledge and consent of the Shah, took to the radio and incited mobs to attack Baha'i places of worship, which resulted in the destruction of the Baha'i community's National Center in Tehran.

With the Islamic Revolution of 1979, the clerical establishment came to power and Iran became a theocracy. The relative calm that the Bahá'ís had enjoyed throughout much of the twentieth century, in which they could, for the most part, make a living and raise their children in peace, was shattered. Bahá'ís again became the target of severe and systematic state-sponsored persecution, and it became official government policy to oppress Bahá'ís. During the Revolution and in the early years afterward, over 200 Bahá'ís were killed, the majority by execution. Thousands were imprisoned, many of them tortured. Bahá'í holy places were destroyed and Bahá'í cemeteries have repeatedly been attacked and desecrated, including the current ongoing excavation of the large Baha'i cemetery in Shiraz.

The government has made concerted efforts to impoverish and quietly suffocate the Bahá'í community. After the Revolution, Bahá'ís were dismissed from government jobs and denied pensions and private employers have been pressured not to hire Bahá'ís. Bahá'ís still suffer frequent raids on their homes and businesses, including a recent spate of shop closures, and their property is routinely seized with compensation. Bahá'ís were also dismissed from university positions after the Revolution, and Bahá'í students continue to be excluded from the nation's universities.

Even the Bahá'i Institute for Higher Education – the informal, volunteer-run network of university-level courses that the Bahá'í community created in the 1980s as an alternative system for its youth – has been the subject of raids and arrests, and twelve educators who volunteered with the Institute are now in prison. Also imprisoned are the "Bahá'í seven" – the seven members of the former ad hoc leadership group of the Bahá'í community, who are now serving 20-year sentences, the longest of any prisoners of conscience in Iran. In total, there are 100 Bahá'ís now imprisoned in Iran, nearly twice the number in 2010. Meanwhile, Bahá'ís continue to be arbitrarily arrested and detained and are often brought up on false charges related to national security and espionage – common charges levelled against anyone who does not hold the same views as the regime.

The clerical establishment in Iran has continued to incite hatred and violence against Bahá'ís. They have long promoted the view that Bahá'ís are ritually unclean. As recently as last month, Hojattul-Islam Reza Karamipour, the Friday prayer leader in the town of Jiroft, stated that, if one shakes hands with a Bahá'i while his hand his damp, he must wash his hands, as they have become ritually unclean – and he exhorted all Muslims to avoid business transactions with Bahá'ís. In 2013, on the eve of the inauguration of President Hassan Rouhani, Supreme Leader Ali Khamenei re-issued a religious decree prohibiting Iranian Muslims from associating with members of the "deviant sect," a well-known reference to Bahá'ís.

All religious minorities in Iran face discrimination and persecution. Unlike Christians, Jews, and Zoroastrians, however, Bahá'ís are not recognized in the Iranian constitution and therefore have no legal status as persons. Under Iranian law, the blood of Bahá'is is mobah, meaning that it can be spilled with impunity. In other words, Bahá'ís can obtain no redress for violent attacks, arson or other types of crimes against them, whether committed by the authorities or by fellow citizens. In August of 2013, Ataollah Rezvani, a Bahá'í in Bandar Abbas was found dead, shot in the head in his car on the outskirts of town. In February of 2014, a Bahá'í family in Birjand was attacked by a masked intruder in their home; all three of them were stabbed, though they fortunately survived. The authorities have not pursued suspects in either case.

In the last several months, there has been a surge in anti-Bahá'í propaganda in state-sponsored media outlets. In 2010 and 2011, approximately 22 anti-Bahá'í pieces were appearing every month. In 2014, the number of anti-Bahá'í pieces rose to approximately 401 per month – eighteen times the previous level.

Next month, Iran will again appear before the United Nations Human Rights Council in Geneva to follow up on the Universal Periodic Review of its human rights record that was conducted in October of 2014. The October session revealed that Iran has failed to live up to dozens of promises to improve human rights that it had made during its last Review in 2010. Eight of these commitments pertained to protecting religious freedom, and four of these eight specifically mentioned the Bahá'ís – including an undertaking to ensure fair trails for the Bahá'í seven, and to fully respect the rights of Bahá'ís. None of these commitments have been honored. On the contrary the human rights situation in Iran has deteriorated in recent years, including for the Bahá'ís. Indeed, the situation has worsened during the year and a half since Iran's new and self-described reformist President, Hassan Rouhani, took office.

Meanwhile, the Iranian government's written response to the October session of the Human Rights Council declared that "[m]inorities, including Baha'is, enjoyed a full range of opportunities and privileges" in Iran. This statement echoes one made last April by the Head of the Iranian Judiciary's Human Rights Council, in which he asserted that "the authorities never target Baha'is just because they are followers of this faith." These statements are, as this document attests, completely contradicted by facts.

The United States government has shown clear leadership in promoting the rights of Bahá'ís and condemning injustice. Since the 1980s, U.S. presidents and other officials have spoken out against the persecution of the Bahá'í community in Iran, and both houses of the U.S. Congress have consistently passed resolutions denouncing the treatment of the Bahá'ís and calling for an end to these continuing abuses. These resolutions and statements, and those that come from other governments around the world, are vital tools in keeping the spotlight on the persecution and raising public awareness of the treatment of Bahá'ís and others in Iran. Because the Iranian government, despite its protestations to the contrary, is quite sensitive to its international image, many observers believe that these efforts have, to some extent, stayed the hand of the Iranian government, and have thereby prevented a bad situation from becoming much worse. In both the domestic and the international arena, the United States government is an essential voice in preventing the escalation of human rights abuses in Iran.

It is our hope that, at the March session of the UN Human Rights Council, the United States and other responsible nations will emphasize the persecution of the Bahá'ís – and the oppression of countless other Iranians – and will hold the Iranian government to account for its gross violations of the human rights of its citizens.

Mr. SMITH. Mr. Vance, thank you so very much for your testimony, and to all of you. We will stand in a brief recess. We have three votes on the floor of the House right now, and then we will resume our sitting of the two subcommittees. But thank you so very much, and I apologize for the inconvenience.

[Recess.]

Ms. ROS-LEHTINEN [presiding]. The subcommittee will come to order. We had a round of votes and Chairman Smith was called for an important meeting, but as soon as he gets done with that he will be back. But thank you for your excellent testimony, and I will begin the question and answer part. Thank you so much.

As I had said in my opening statement, despite the administration's lip service to the issue of human rights, they have been effectively ignoring human rights in our foreign policy discussion and implementation to the detriment of millions who are suffering under tyranny. As we know, actions speak louder than words and this administration has thrown human rights to the back burner, especially in places like my native homeland of Cuba and in Iran where the administration has been desperate to secure deals with these tyrannical regimes.

So I am sorry if I am not going to pronounce your names correctly, but I have a very difficult name as well and I don't get upset when people don't know how to say it.

Mr. Arya?

Mr. ARYA. Arya.

Ms. ROS-LEHTINEN. Arya. You testified that human rights have "been overlooked by the international community in light of current negotiations between Iran and the P5+1." How has the human rights situation in Iran changed in these negotiations under Rouhani?

Mr. ARYA. Well, Madam Chairman, as I said it is getting worse. I mean if you look at the Islamic regime, it is in their nature when they feel secure they just become aggressive. When they see that there is no attention being paid to the issue of human rights, for example, they just do whatever they want and they see no reason why they should stop. They get rid of their opponents, they do all kinds of things that is just true to their nature.

But everything has gotten worse and all the statistics show that everything has gotten worse, from the number of executions, from the number of juveniles being executed, from religious minorities, everything has been worse under Rouhani. And my take, I think, is that international community hasn't paid enough attention to this issue, and they haven't been forcing Rouhani to stand up to his campaign promises and things of that nature. They just focus on the nuclear issue and then push everything aside. So that is unfortunate, I believe, that everything has gotten worse, and it is time for international community and U.S. administration especially to pay attention to that issue as well.

Ms. ROS-LEHTINEN. Well, I agree. And I see such similarities in my native homeland of Cuba when on December 17th the President announced we will have diplomatic relations with the Castro regime. And tomorrow another round of negotiations will take place in the State Department and the lead negotiator for that agreement is Josefina Vidal who was a spy for Cuba and was actually expelled by the United States because of her espionage activities, now she is in charge of the negotiations.

What signal does that tell the Castro regime? We can do whatever we want and everything is forgiven, and it sends a terrible signal to the human rights activists. That is why it comes as no surprise that since the President's announcement on December 17th, there has been a record number of arrests in Cuba. You would think that at the very least Raul Castro would tone this down while people are paying attention, but the sad fact is, as you pointed out, people are not paying attention.

And so if the United States does not lead the way, the international community will be silent. They will be silent in Cuba. They were silent in Venezuela. And they are silent in Iran. That is why the United States has such a pivotal role to play when it comes to talking about human rights and doing something about human rights. Because if not, it sends a message to Rouhani that he can do whatever he wants, keep executing people, keep jailing people for their religious beliefs, we will look the other way.

And that sends a chilling message to so many people living under this yoke of tyranny in Iran who want to be free, who want a different kind of government, but they think, well, obviously no one is paying attention, and the international community, they are so eager to have this nuclear deal that they are willing to look the other way as well.

What kind of support do you see for the issue of Iranian human rights internationally in human rights organizations, et cetera?

Mr. ARYA. Well, I believe that on every arena from the administration to the Congress, this issue should be brought up continuously. In the United Nations, everywhere. Because without that the Islamic regime won't do anything then. I mean they will continue to abuse the Iranian people's rights.

A very good example, if I may, the way President Reagan dealt with Gorbachev, they wanted to make a deal with Gorbachev, they had good relationship with Gorbachev. They negotiated with him. They did all of that. But at the same time, when President Reagan went to Moscow he made a point to meet with the dissidents. And that sent a very good message, encouraging message, to all the anti-Soviet dissidents all over the former Soviet Union.

Ms. ROS-LEHTINEN. That they were not forgotten.

Mr. ARYA. Exactly.

Ms. ROS-LEHTINEN. People cared about them.

Mr. ARYA. Exactly. The attitude of U.S. and European countries and all the other countries should be the same way. That whatever negotiations that goes between, I mean we understand. I am a member of opposition. I advocate regime change in Iran. But at the same time I understand that international relations and security concerns dictates that sometimes they have to negotiate with the Islamic regime. That is fine. But at the same time that negotiation, that improvement in relationship should not come at the expense of Iranian people's rights to freedom. That is the most important——

Ms. ROS-LEHTINEN. It is not an either/or.

Mr. ARYA. Exactly.

Ms. ROS-LEHTINEN. And yet we give that message to the people with whom we are dealing whether it is Rouhani, whether it is Castro. They will say, well, we are just going to talk about diplomatic relations with Cuba, we will ignore human rights. We are just going to talk about a nuclear deal with Rouhani, we will ignore human rights. And that is a great boost to these regimes to keep harassing, intimidating and jailing opposition leaders because they have actually been given a green light to do so by our very own Government.

Mr. ARYA. I agree.

Ms. ROS-LEHTINEN. Mr. Sazegara?

Mr. SAZEGARA. Yes.

Ms. ROS-LEHTINEN. Thank you. You were one of the founding members of the Islamic Revolutionary Guard Corps before being imprisoned for your opposition to the regime. What can you tell us about the inner workings of the IRGC and the Iranian regime, its financing capabilities and the risk that the IRGC poses to U.S. interests and to our regional security interest?

Mr. SAZEGARA. I was one of the founders of the Revolutionary Guard and one of the writers of the Charter of Revolutionary Guard in the first 3 months of victory of revolution, and then I left the guard and went to the National Radio and Television of Iran. But I followed the changes in the Revolutionary Guard during the last 36 years.

Right now the Revolutionary Guard is, I believe, a kind of unique organization and maybe all around the world, because at the same time Revolutionary Guard is like a political party, a terrorist organization, a mafia group involved in the smuggling of drugs, alcoholic beverages, sex traffic in Iran, and a complex holding company. It owns several companies, huge manufacturing and trading companies of Iran. And its intelligence organization which directly works under command of son of the Ayatollah, the leader of Iran, is more brutal than Ministry of Intelligence and more powerful.

So a part of at least the most important part of the nuclear project of Iran is controlled by the Revolutionary Guard as well. Besides that I think that especially these coming years, I mean 2015 and 2016, because of illness of the leader, the political competition in Iran amongst several factions especially inside the Revolutionary Guard will be increased. And for this simple reason, as a political activist I am really, really afraid of more brutality, more separation of the people during this year and the year after.

And the economic crisis which has been created not only because of the sanctions, more than the sanctions are mismanagement and oil price, which has been decreased about 60 percent, and several other factors will affect several aspects of Iranian people on this year.

And again, riots, strikes, protests of workers, of teachers, I believe that we will suffer brutality by Revolutionary Guard this year and the year after. I want to add——

Ms. ROS-LEHTINEN. In Iran itself.

Mr. SAZEGARA. Yes.

Ms. ROS-LEHTINEN. And what about the risks that they pose for our interests and regional concerns?

Mr. SAZEGARA. As you know, the Quds Force of Revolutionary Guard, which has about 14,000 members, is the special division of Revolutionary Guard which is in charge of out-of-Iran operations. I think that because of the internal affairs of Iran, the Quds Force of Revolutionary Guard will increase the out-of-Iran operations and adventurism in the region.

And I say adventurism because they know from the period of war between Iran and Iraq that in crisis and military situation and in out-of-Iran crisis they can have the upper hand in internal politics. For instance, recently the missile platforms in Golan Heights, which were attacked by Israelis and destroyed, as far as I know there are several projects like that in the whole region, or assassination of some prominent opposition figures outside Iran by new methods that they hire some thugs to attack them just by knives or daggers or something like that, the example that happened in Jerusalem 2 or 3 months ago, or other crises.

I mean I expect for the year coming acceleration of out-of-Iran operations, terrorist operations, and creating some conflicts too because of, especially because of the internal competitions in Iran.

Ms. ROS-LEHTINEN. To take away attention from their inner problems, have they focused on that?

Mr. SAZEGARA. And they know that in such situations they become more powerful in internal politics if they say that yes we are involved in Iraq. This is the war over there in Yemen, with Israel, especially with Israel, in the border of Israel, or Hezbollah Lebanon involvement in some battles against Israel or several others that, other operations that they have done so far. They can have the upper hand in internal politics as well.

I want to add to Mr. Arya's that as far as I know, Mr. Kerry has agreed with Mr. Zarif to put any human rights issue off the table. That is what, at the first terms of the rounds of negotiations Zarif has said that if you bring any human rights issue on the table, then Ayatollah Khamenei will order us to leave the table. So they have confidence that there will be no pressure——

Ms. ROS-LEHTINEN. They don't have to worry about it.

Mr. SAZEGARA. Yes.

Ms. ROS-LEHTINEN. It will be off the table.

Mr. SAZEGARA. Iranians watch the U.S. policies through some windows like Voice of America, and unfortunately on these days they don't hear anything even from Voice of America. And the regime sells the idea to the people that see, we have behind a curtain——

Ms. ROS-LEHTINEN. We are fine.

Mr. SAZEGARA. We have the agreement and nobody can help you. You look at that. There is nothing to say about that.

Ms. ROS-LEHTINEN. And the opposition feels dispirited. Well, thank you very much. I appreciate it.

Mr. Vance, the regime's treatment of Baha'is is getting worse under Rouhani, not better. Can you describe the treatment and the abuse of Baha'is under Rouhani and what does the persecution of the Baha'is in Iran mean for human rights in general? And what more can you tell me about the prisoner of conscience that I had adopted, Rozita Vaseghi, her health, her current situation, including the likelihood that Iranian authorities will try to imprison her again? Thank you, sir.

Mr. VANCE. Sure. Thank you, Madam Chairman.

Well, we had been, first, we were guardedly optimistic when President Rouhani was elected that he would actually improve the situation, especially since he had promised, one of his election promises was to put together a draft charter of citizens' rights and have it circulated and finalized. He did actually issue a draft in November 2013.

Ms. ROS-LEHTINEN. Oh, you should read the Cuban Constitution. It is a beauty. They don't follow one word of it, but it is beautiful.

Mr. VANCE. We were very disappointed with the draft because it made all of the rights under it contingent on the Iranian Constitution and on Iranian law. So it didn't actually hold out any promise for any future improvements. And I think the draft got a great deal of pushback and criticism from a number of circles, so it has never been actually circulated again, to the best of our knowledge. And that, I think, signaled what we were beginning to see, and that is that one of the trends—we have always had Baha'is who have been harassed, raids on homes, raids on businesses. The amount of physical abuse in those raids has actually increased over the last couple of years and certainly has not decreased under President Rouhani. Baha'is have, because they are excluded from so many professions in Iran, they have become largely small business people running their own small businesses. And there is a very large amount of economic harassment refusing either to provide or renew business licenses, closing shops arbitrarily.

In October, for example, on October 25th, in Kerman and a couple of other cities nearby, there were 79 shops that were closed simply because the shopkeepers had observed a Baha'i holy day. And so the shops were actually sealed. But perhaps the most disturbing thing that has occurred, at least in my opinion, is the increase in hate propaganda. Because it has been shown in many societies that it is a prerequisite, or at least it presages in many societies a much more serious crackdown on the population that is being targeted.

I had mentioned that, in 2014, there were 18 times the number of anti-Baha'i articles, not just criticizing Baha'is but portraying them as being agents of the United States, agents of Russia, agents of Israel, accusing them of all sorts of immorality. It is all designed to create a sense in people's minds that persecution of Baha'is is justified.

So based on the very unfortunate history of good portions of the twentieth century, I am much more concerned about that than any other single factor. And certainly that would be in the control of, all of this is state-sponsored media and that is certainly within the control or should be in the control of President Rouhani.

So we are concerned about that. We are concerned that for human rights in general in Iran, because the Baha'is are the largest non-Muslim religious minority in the country and because they have been traditionally despised to a greater degree than any other group by the Muslim clergy, we know that if things were to improve for the Baha'is, they would improve for everybody because it is inconceivable that things could get better for the Baha'is in Iran without them also getting better for other groups. So in a sense we are that barometer, let us say, of what, how we are being treated is a barometer for the rest of the civil society.

And as to Rozita Vaseghi, we are delighted that she was released from prison in Mashhad on January 21st. You had noted earlier that she is uncertain as to what her future is because she had two 5-year sentences and it was unclear whether they were going to be successive or concurrent. The way things stand at the moment they were concurrent. They released her.

But she was also told that she might have another 2-year sentence, and so we don't know what is going to happen with that. She certainly has health problems that have to be dealt with, and rather than get into the details of that I can simply say that 5 years in prison in Mashhad took a definite health toll on her. Thank you.

Ms. ROS-LEHTINEN. Which was one of the objectives of the regime. Thank you very much. Excellent, excellent answers. We appreciate it.

Mr. Cicilline?

Mr. CICILLINE. Thank you, Madam Chair.

Thank you again for your very, very important testimony. I think it is very clear to anyone that has looked at this issue that the human rights abuses in Iran are horrific and are contrary to basic American values and universal values of human rights. And I think the challenge for us is to determine what is the most effective way for us to try to change that as responsible world leaders and part of the international community.

And so my first question really is, is there any sense that President Rouhani, even if he were inclined to change his view on human rights, would be empowered to actually make substantial changes in the condition of basic human rights in Iran, or is the Supreme Leader responsible for this set of practices such that the President wouldn't actually have the ability or the capacity to change it? Because I think it is important to kind of know where our leverage points should be in the conversation to begin. I don't know if anyone has a sense of that.

Mr. SAZEGARA. According to the Constitution of Islamic Republic, President is the head of the executive power. And judiciary power is controlled by the leader, the head of judiciary power is appointed by the leader, and all the judges and prosecutors are appointed by that head.

And Rouhani just theoretically doesn't have so much power to change some parts of these human rights abuses in Iran, but at least he can do something. For instance, changing his Minister of Justice, a notorious killer, a notorious person to violate human rights and in charge of massacre, or he can put pressure on keeping the freedom of press in Iran, because the Ministry of Culture and Islamic Guidance is in charge of the press and it is controlled by Rouhani, but he doesn't do that. Or changing the situation, for instance, in Iranian universities with respect to teachers' associations, labor associations, but he has not done anything with respect to these parts.

He can do something to help the civil society of Iran to confront the suppression of the rights of the people of Iran, but so far he has not done anything. And even he has not said anything about the home arrest of the leaders of Green Movement of Iran or the other political prisoners.

So I believe that some parts of the violations has happened by the hands of the Minister of Intelligence, while the Minister of Intelligence is a member of the cabinet. So I think that yes, although he is not directly in charge of the judiciary power, he can do many things by the tools that he has in the executive power, by the people, by the civil society of Iran and support at least the basic freedoms of people of Iran, but he has not done anything.

Mr. ARYA. I would like to add I agree with Mr. Sazegara as well, however, I believe it is a mistake to believe, to think of Rouhani as someone separated from the whole totality of the regime. As I said, he has been part of this regime from the beginning and he has been serving this regime at the highest levels, security levels, from the beginning until now. So it is foolhardy to me that we think of him as an outsider who wanted to come and do some reforms. He may have presented himself during the election as such or to the international community that he really is trying to make things better, but things are not really in his hands. The judicial system is not really in my hands, the security system is not really in my hand, this is not in my hand, that is not in my hand, all I can do is this and that.

But he is part of this regime. I mean he has been approving—I mean the Mr. Shariatmadari is the notorious editor of Kayhan, a very hardline, radical newspaper in Iran. He said it and I agree with him. He said that what is all this—and I am paraphrasing. He said what is all this talk about him wanting to release the leaders of the Green Movement, Mr. Mousavi, Mr. Rahnavard, and Mr. Karroubi? He said he voted for their imprisonment. At the National Security Council he voted for them to be incarcerated. What is this all talk about? I mean to me it is a mistake to think of him separately.

Mr. CICILLINE. And is there any evidence that you have seen that international pressure that may have been made on the human rights abuses as having any effect on the regime? Would you talk a little bit about it? Yes.

Mr. SAZEGARA. Yes, yes, definitely.

Mr. CICILLINE. And so things like this hearing I assume are helpful because they are helping to bring attention to this issue. Similarly, if we were to enact a comprehensive statement of our kind of affirmation of basic human rights, would that be useful? Yes, okay.

Mr. SAZEGARA. Yes, I can mention several cases including my case. I was in confines for 79 days. I was on a long hunger strike. And 800 students were arrested with me when they arrested me including my son who was a university student in those days. And international pressure was really, really effective to release not only me but all those students.

And I think that more than just telling, and just by statements of that, something like Helsinki Accord, something which happened that put real pressure on the Communist bloc. Right now the sanctions has worked. They have brought the regime to the negotiation table. If we can use at least a part of these sanctions targeted to human rights, I believe, at least the people who are in charge of the violation of human rights in Iran be under sanction, I think that it works. And the letter soon will send the right signal to the people of Iran that the international community is concerned and puts real pressure on this regime.

Mr. ARYA. May I add something? I agree. And one thing I would really like to, if anything I would like to relay in this hearing is that Islamic regime only responds to force. Not just military force, but when they see that the international community is standing up firmly on any issue they eventually back off.

In Europe during the 1980s and 1990s, more than 200 Iranian dissidents were assassinated all over Europe. European countries kind of looked the other way. They said, well, it is this element of a radical group in the regime or that group, and it didn't stop. It only stopped when after the massacre in Mykonos all the European countries got together, they pulled back their Ambassadors and they imposed some sanctions. Since then there hasn't been any assassinations that I know of. So they respond to firmness and united front, they will respond to that. Otherwise they will just do whatever they want.

Mr. CICILLINE. I just ask the chair if I might just ask the last two things. If you would speak to the current situation for members of the LGBT community in Iran, specifically are there concerns about the basic human rights of lesbian, gay, bisexual, and transgender community, and also if you could speak to any information you might have about Jason Rezaian, if I am pronouncing his name correctly, who is an American journalist and who was detained and has been detained. I understand that he hasn't been able to have his defense counsel meet with him, and whether or not there are current efforts underway that you are aware of to secure his release.

Mr. SAZEGARA. As far as I know about Jason Rezaian, he has been kept in a confined cell and under pressure for TV confessions. And they have taped a TV confession from him that he is an agent of CIA and the secret services, and he has——

Mr. CICILLINE. This is the Washington Post correspondent, just for the people, yes.

Mr. SAZEGARA. Yes. And the Revolutionary Guard has done that. And he has confessed that one of the relatives of Rouhani in his office has helped him and his connection, so they have made something out of his confessions to put pressure on Rouhani for internal clashes in the regime.

So I know that Jason Rezaian is just a journalist and has not done anything, but this is what they do, how they behave. This is what they call it to make a scenario out of any political prisoner. So they have a TV confession from him, and I doubt that they finish this case easily unless you have a very, very heavy pressure on the regime.

Mr. ARYA. I have nothing to add to that.

Mr. CICILLINE. And with respect to the LGBT community?

Mr. ARYA. LGBT community are again it is against Sharia law, being gay, and they are under enormous pressure. The only group that I know of that are not kind of tolerated, if they want to go through sex change then they have provisions to allow that. But that is only a small group of LGBT community. If somebody is gay and wants to remain gay and wants to be lesbian or remain lesbian without going through sex change and things like that they will be persecuted. I mean I don't exactly know the time, but recently they told two gay men—just punish them, to kill them as part of the punishment prescribed in Sharia for gay people.

So I don't see any kind of light in the end of the tunnel for that community in Iran so long as the Islamic regime is in power because they won't tolerate it. Because it goes against everything that they claim to stand by, so it undermines their legitimacy, undermines their claim of legitimacy in terms of religious doctrine that they prescribe to. I see no improvement in their situation except that small little group who want to go through the sex change. Other than that they are in terrible shape just like any other.

Mr. CICILLINE. Thank you very much again, and I thank the chair.

Ms. ROS-LEHTINEN. Thank you very much.

Mr. DeSantis?

Mr. DESANTIS. Thank you Madam Chairman.

Mr. Sazegara, when you joined the Islamic Revolution in 1979, you were there it seemed to be from, I read your bio, about 10 years before you left?

Mr. SAZEGARA. Yes.

Mr. DESANTIS. 1988, is that when you left government?

Mr. SAZEGARA. Yes.

Mr. DESANTIS. So did you change or was it the regime that changed?

Mr. SAZEGARA. Both.

Mr. DESANTIS. So at the time you were, in 1979, because as I remember that time or think about the time, I was just a kid but there was dissatisfaction with the Shah, but there were a lot of people who didn't want an Islamic Revolution. They wanted a secular revolution. They just didn't want to have that ruling elite in power, and then obviously you had the Mullahs who wanted a Sharia revolution. So were you expecting a Sharia revolution or did you just think you would remove the Shah and have a chance to have a better Iran?

Mr. SAZEGARA. Better to say that everybody on those days, the majority of the people, 35 million Iranian population those days, everybody was eager to have a revolution, an ideological revolution. At least the university educated people like me, we didn't think that an Islamic regime would be based on Sharia and the Mullahs would get all the power.

In those days we were affected by leftists, and a version of Islam that I can call a revolutionary, ideological version of Islam was dominant in the Islamic movement and was effective to mobilize the people against Shah. But gradually after victory of revolution, the Mullahs got the upper hand by of course the leader of revolution, Ayatollah Khomenei who was a Grand Ayatollah. And gradually other factions of anti-Shah movement were dismissed, were suppressed, were massacred, during one decade. So anybody who didn't agree with them was under pressure.

I personally, the change that, my changes were not only in this part from the theoretical point of view but in action, because for 4 or 5 years I was the head of the biggest industrial complex of

Iran which owns about 140 huge manufacturing companies of Iran. And in practice I found out that many policies that we thought to run the country on were wrong as well, so I gradually——

Mr. DeSANTIS. So it was a perfect storm for you.

Mr. SAZEGARA. Yes, I left the regime in 1988.

Mr. DeSANTIS. So what did you think when the Ayatollah started to fund and support groups like Hezbollah in Lebanon that would conduct terrorist attacks?

Mr. SAZEGARA. It had started from the first decade. The idea of exportation of revolution was born with the revolution, like many other revolutions of course.

Mr. DeSANTIS. And so that was a natural outgrowth to have outposts in Lebanon where you would have people who could conduct operations?

Mr. SAZEGARA. Yes, and especially that several activists of the Islamic Revolution were trained in Lebanon and they lived in Lebanon for several years. And if precisely I can say it had started from an Office of Liberation Movements All Around the World in the Revolutionary Guard in 1981–1982, and gradually it was changed to Quds Corps and later it became Quds Force which were in charge of organizations like Hezbollah in Lebanon.

Mr. DeSANTIS. So an attack such as the attack that was conducted on the U.S. Marines in Beirut in 1983, that would have been just a basic application of their revolutionary mindset, correct?

Mr. SAZEGARA. Yes.

Mr. DeSANTIS. So let me ask you now, fast forward, clearly this regime is one of the most repressive in the world. There was a chance it seemed in 2009 with the Green Movement where there were a lot of people who were really brave to express their dissatisfaction.

The administration here in the United States made the decision that that was not something that they wanted to support. I think the reason was because they thought that that would jeopardize their ability to have a constructive relationship with the Ayatollah.

The President has written the Ayatollah a number of letters. I think that was a mistake. I think that we need to be supporting groups who are challenging the regime and standing up for human rights in Iran. Do you agree that the United States should have been supportive of the Green Movement?

Mr. SAZEGARA. Yes. Still I wear this green wristband. On that summer, summer of 2009, I was in Washington, DC, and I was one of the activists of the Green Movement. We had several meetings with the officials of administrations, but yes, you are right. No support. And in those days we didn't know that behind the curtain they are writing some letters to the leader of Iran——

Mr. DeSANTIS. Right.

Mr. SAZEGARA [continuing]. And some communications. But we didn't get any real support. And besides to that on those days I was on a weekly TV show in Voice of America, a talk show, which was very effective in the movement because we had the connection with the leaders of the movement. Not the leaders, the activists of the movement, and we could give information about the demonstrations, what is going on, and we had real problems in the Voice of

America as well. I mean lots of pressure in the Voice of America. And at last that program was stopped.

Mr. DeSantis. I have been frustrated, and I know that my friend from Florida, the chairman, has mentioned this that there is this, really, just lust to kind of have a kind of ''deal'' about these nukes. And a lot of us don't think that is going to be effective, but it will allow the administration to wave a sheet of paper. But because they are so eager bending over backwards to try to get a deal, they are really turning a blind eye to some of these human rights problems even more so than they had been doing previously.

But with respect to this deal, Iran is one of the most energy-rich countries in the world. What do they need nuclear power for in terms of for peaceful purposes? I mean it just seems to me that you could see like France or some of these other countries that don't have access to energy, they have hundreds of years of energy reserves and they haven't even started fracking yet. So are you skeptical that they will use it for peaceful purposes?

Mr. Sazegara. Yes, very much. I think that so far Iran has spent billions of dollars in this project and the value of whatever they have produced is just a couple of million dollars. And definitely it is not feasible to produce nuclear energy in Iran. Iran has the biggest supplies of natural gas in the world. Yes, definitely.

Mr. DeSantis. Mr. Arya?

Mr. Arya. May I add something to this? I think you should look at Islamic regime and its drive to this nuclear issue from the perspective of their security. I believe that they want this program for several reasons and they won't give it up. One is that if they go nuclear they have something to show to their own supporters. And yes, the economy is bad, yes, your lives are terrible, all that stuff, but look at the end, we made Iran an atomic, nuclear power. The second thing that they look for in my opinion is that they believe that if they get the bomb they have secured the regime.

Mr. DeSantis. Right.

Mr. Sazegara. Just like North Korea, nobody will be able to do anything. And that security is twofold. One is from outside threat; one is internal. I certainly believe that they in their minds and in their hearts' calculations they think that if they get the bomb they will be secure from outside threat, and internally if there is a big, huge uprising they can do anything they want without nobody being able to do anything. They can massacre hundreds of thousands of people and nobody will be able to do anything.

So because of all these calculations, otherwise it doesn't make sense that they spend all this time, all this money, enduring all these sanctions that have damaged the Iranian economy to the point of almost collapse, hundreds and hundreds of billions of dollars damage to this economy for what? For generating power? It doesn't make sense. They want it for military application. If not they don't want it to make it maybe today or tomorrow, but they want to be so close to it that they will have that option anytime they want and they want to choose.

And that is a security thing in their minds, in the mind of the Supreme Leader and the security apparatus around him, and all the Revolutionary Guard people who are controlling everything in

Iran these days. They look at it as an insurance policy that they will use it for saving their own regime. That is——

Mr. DeSantis. And so if you have freedom fighters and people who want to have an Iran in which individual liberty is respected, Iran has an advantageous deal where they can go nuclear, you are making it way more difficult that those forces of progress will succeed, correct?

Mr. Arya. Exactly.

Mr. DeSantis. One final. In terms of the nuclear ambitions, I agree with you. I mean it defies logic that they would do this stuff unless they wanted a military application. Because the losses that they have incurred to use it for peaceful energy, I mean they have the energy, and so you are 100 percent right about that.

And I agree with you about the insurance aspect, and there are a lot of reasons why they would want to do it. What about the offensive use of nuclear weapons? People have said that they have said over and over again that they would like to eliminate Israel from the map. They obviously say death to America a lot.

And while there are other countries who may be hostile to our allies or to us, we do have this deterrent capability, because obviously we have nuclear weapons and other countries may have them, but in the case of Iran, if they could take a potshot and take out Tel Aviv, let's say, and kill millions of Jews, they know they would get hit on return in Tehran or wherever and lose maybe more than a few million Iranians. But from their ideology they would say that they are hastening the return maybe of the Twelfth Imam, the people who are killed in Iran would be going straight to paradise.

So do you think that them with nukes with that ideology, is that something that is a little bit different from some of the other nuclear powers that we have seen in the past whether it is the Soviet Union, whether it is North Korea, which is crazy but they do want to keep themselves in power, and they are Communists so they don't believe in an afterlife.

Mr. Arya. There definitely is that aspect to it. I mean they are, I mean some elements within that regime they are not really rational people. And all those calculations may come into their play and that is why it is very dangerous for them to have that nuclear capability in terms of military application. However, if you look at the Islamic regime, whenever they have felt that they have the upper hand and whenever they have felt that they are secure they have gone aggressive. Their behavior has changed.

I mean you look at from the very beginning, you look at the hostage crisis when they took over the American Embassy. The hostage takers, they admit that they only wanted to take the hostages for a couple of days, 3 or 4 days, to send a message and they will release them. As soon as the regime establishment, Khomenei and people around him, realized that the Carter administration is not going to do anything and it is safe to keep them, they kept them for 444 days.

Iran-Iraq War, in 1982, Iranian forces liberated Khorramshahr. They pushed all the Iraqi forces back. At that time Iran was at the highest military position and Iraq was afraid, all the Arab countries in the Persian Gulf were afraid that Iran will enter the Iraqi territory. At that time everybody offered them all kinds of incentives to accept a ceasefire. They felt powerful. They didn't do that. They continued on. They marched on into Iraq, and they only accepted the ceasefire when they had nothing left basically. Even Mr. Rezaee at one point in one of his interviews admitted that had the war continued for another week they wouldn't even have ammunitions for their handguns. So they push all the way there.

The same thing in Lebanon, in Syria, in Iraq and now in Yemen. You look at their behavior in Iraq. As soon as, I mean there is a very wonderful article in the New York Times about how this whole thing unfolded in Iraq, when after 9/11 they were extremely afraid that somehow America will go after them and they started cooperating with Ambassador Crocker. They tried to be nice to him and gave him some information and stuff. As soon as U.S. went into Iraq and they realized that there is no plan to move into Iran or do anything about their regime, they went aggressive and they caused all that chaos in Iraq.

Mr. DeSantis. They were responsible for killing hundreds of U.S. service members.

Mr. Arya. Exactly. Why do they do that? Because as soon as they feel secure, as soon as they feel that there is no repercussions for their actions they go aggressive. And they have showed it time and time and time again. If they ever get their hands on a nuclear bomb, if you think that they are aggressive now, wait until then. They won't even need to use that bomb to blow up Tel Aviv or anywhere else.

There are hundreds of other things they can do to make life miserable not only for Israelis but for the whole region, as they have done so. I mean look at Syria, look at Iraq. I mean the carnage that they have caused is immeasurable, I mean in Iraq and everywhere.

Mr. DeSantis. So what in the Congress, and everyone can opine on this. What do you recommend that we do? I know there are things geopolitically with how we would confront Iran and some of their proxies. But in terms of empowering opposition, empowering people who want a different, a better Iran, because I definitely know that although the regime is one of the most oppressive in the world there are millions of Iranians who are chafing under this and I think could be natural allies of ours. So what do you recommend that the Congress can do to empower those elements and ultimately to make Iran a better place?

Mr. Arya. If you ask me, sir, the best thing that U.S. can do is get rid of this mentality of betting on the winning horse, per se. We need to identify people who are truly democratic and they are truly in line with our values in the West and just support them, give them platforms. Not necessarily money or anything, but just like give them platforms to express their views.

I always think about Germany after World War II. In Germany, we in the U.S. just did and stood by helping everybody. They identified democratic forces within German society. They gave them financial support. They gave them political support. They gave them moral support. They gave them all kinds of assistance. And gradually say Christian Democrats, they started to grow and grow and grow and become more and more powerful. So that is the thing. Right now, for example, all this, the U.S. administration's attempt to say, use Quds Forces against ISIS, is just, it is ridiculous to me. I am sorry to say that but it is ridiculous. I mean to defeat one radical and to replace it with another radical, you don't gain anything.

The best thing for the U.S. is to identify people who are truly aligned with our values in the West and give them moral support, give them platforms to expand their ideas. Right now in Voice of America, for example, and Mr. Sazegara mentioned it, a lot of moderate groups don't even get a chance to go over there and express their ideas. It is almost impossible to do.

That is the best thing that U.S. Congress can do. Stand by democratic forces, promote them and give them encouragement, and stay away from all the other radicals whom we can use for short period of time, because that hasn't paid off. It just replaces one bad guy with another bad guy. And then in the process, the ordinary people they just blame America. They say hey, look at them. They are playing with us in order just, it is all a big game.

The conspiracy theories are wild in the Middle East. They look at it and say, okay, well, America is using ISIS against Iran and Iran against ISIS. So this is just all a game for America. We should stay away from it. We should stand by people who are truly in line with our values. That is all I can say, sir.

Mr. DeSantis. You guys want to chime in? What do you advise us to do?

Mr. Sazegara. I have submitted a proposal, the appendix to my testimony. I kindly ask you to read that. And in that proposal I have suggested to have a standing subcommittee for human rights in Iran to watch very carefully the human rights and show that the Congress of the United States is concerned about the human rights in Iran.

And put pressure on the sources of money of the institutions and the persons who abuse human rights in Iran, who violate human rights in Iran. The first person is the leader and then Revolutionary Guard and several other institutions. Forty percent of Iran's economy is controlled by these organizations.

So Ayatollah Khamenei, the leader, insists that human rights should be off the table of any negotiation. I think Congress can put on the table, if not in this negotiation, the nuclear negotiation, in other commissions and say that okay, these sanctions will not be removed or new sanctions will be regulated in Congress to keep the hands of the suppression groups and forces in Iran off the people in Iran. So I think that this is the real force that they understand and will send a good signal to the people of Iran that the United States is concerned about their rights and their freedoms.

Mr. DeSantis. Mr. Vance, you want to weigh in?

Mr. Vance. We don't actually have any specific recommendations, so certainly we have been grateful for the resolutions that have usually been passed in each Congress that highlight the situation with respect to human rights and especially the Baha'is in Iran, but we don't have any recommendations on U.S. policy.

Mr. DeSantis. Great. Well, I appreciate the witnesses. Really a lot of good information and a lot of good insights. So I thank you for coming.

Ms. ROS-LEHTINEN. Thank you so much, Mr. DeSantis, for your deep interest in this important issue. Very good questions and excellent answers from our panelists.

Unfortunately our subcommittee chairman, Mr. Smith, has been unavoidably detained, so with that our joint subcommittee hearing is now adjourned. Thank you to all.

[Whereupon, at 4:20 p.m., the subcommittee was adjourned.]

APPENDIX

MATERIAL SUBMITTED FOR THE RECORD

JOINT SUBCOMMITTEE HEARING NOTICE
COMMITTEE ON FOREIGN AFFAIRS
U.S. HOUSE OF REPRESENTATIVES
WASHINGTON, DC 20515-6128

Subcommittee on Africa, Global Health, Global Human Rights, and International Organizations
Christopher H. Smith (R-NJ), Chairman

Subcommittee on the Middle East and North Africa
Ileana Ros-Lehtinen (R-FL), Chairman

February 26, 2015

TO: MEMBERS OF THE COMMITTEE ON FOREIGN AFFAIRS

You are respectfully requested to attend an OPEN hearing of the Committee on Foreign Affairs, to be held jointly by the Subcommittee on Africa, Global Health, Global Human Rights, and International Organizations and the Subcommittee on the Middle East and North Africa in Room 2172 of the Rayburn House Office Building (and available live on the Committee website at http://www.ForeignAffairs.house.gov):

DATE: Thursday, February 26, 2015

TIME: 2:00 p.m.

SUBJECT: The Shame of Iranian Human Rights

WITNESSES: Mr. Shayan Arya
Central Committee Member
Constitutionalist Party of Iran (Liberal Democrat)

Mr. Mohsen Sazegara
President
Research Institute on Contemporary Iran

Mr. Anthony Vance
Director
U.S. Baha'i Office of Public Affairs

By Direction of the Chairman

The Committee on Foreign Affairs seeks to make its facilities accessible to persons with disabilities. If you are in need of special accommodations, please call 202/225-5021 at least four business days in advance of the event, whenever practicable. Questions with regard to special accommodations in general (including availability of Committee materials in alternative formats and assistive listening devices) may be directed to the Committee.

COMMITTEE ON FOREIGN AFFAIRS

MINUTES OF SUBCOMMITTEE ON ___Africa, Global Health, Global Human Rights, and International Organizations / the Middle East and North Africa___ HEARING

Day___ *Thursday*___ Date___ *February 26, 2015*___ Room___ *2172 Rayburn HOB*___

Starting Time___ *2:00 p.m.*___ Ending Time___ *4:20 p.m.*___

Recesses | *1* | (*2:49* to *3:20*) (___to___) (___to___) (___to___) (___to___) (___to___)

Presiding Member(s)

Rep. Chris Smith, Rep. Ilena Ros-Lehtinen

Check all of the following that apply:

Open Session ☑   Electronically Recorded (taped) ☑
Executive (closed) Session ☐   Stenographic Record ☑
Televised ☑

TITLE OF HEARING:

The Shame of Iranian Human Rights

SUBCOMMITTEE MEMBERS PRESENT:

AGH: Rep. David Cicilline
MENA: Rep. Theodore Deutch, Rep. Darrell Issa, Rep. Steve Chabot, Rep. Dave Trott, Rep. Gerald Connolly, Rep. Ron DeSantis

---

NON-SUBCOMMITTEE MEMBERS PRESENT: *(Mark with an * if they are not members of full committee.)*

HEARING WITNESSES: Same as meeting notice attached? Yes ☑ No ☐
(If "no", please list below and include title, agency, department, or organization.)

STATEMENTS FOR THE RECORD: *(List any statements submitted for the record.)*

Proposals of Mr. Moshen Sazegara, submitted by Mr. Moshen Sazegara

---

TIME SCHEDULED TO RECONVENE _____
or
TIME ADJOURNED___ *4:20 p.m.*___

Gregory B. Simpkins
Subcommittee Staff Director

Appendix

A Proposal to form a Standing Subcommittee for Human Rights in Iran
under the Subcommittee on the Middle East and North Africa
and
Two initial Proposals for its Docket

Standing Subcommittee for Human Rights in Iran

Iran has been in violation of a huge number of its international obligations. Extensive and systematic human rights abuse and brutal crackdown of its dissidents is an example of such violations of international rules. There are a number of official and unofficial groups and individuals who follow and monitor human rights abuses in Iran. Due to the gravity of such abuses in Iran in terms of both frequency and nature, **it is hereby submitted that a Standing Subcommittee be formed under the Subcommittee on the Middle East and North Africa.** This body would be a central coordination point for monitoring, processing and communicating the Iranian regime's human rights abuses to the US legislature and decision-makers, and for suggesting proposals to help prevent or at least mitigate such abuses in Iran.

Human rights abuses in Iran are huge. In order to have a clearer picture about Iran's pervasive violations of international obligations, suffice it to skim through the Pax Americana Institute's report prepared in 2011, and the Annual Analytic-Statistics Reports of Human Rights Violation in Iran in 2013 and 2014, as well as the UN Special Rapporteur's Reports. The first report renders an accurate and well-substantiated, yet non-comprehensive, facts and arguments about such violations under three topics: **Nuclear Program and Proliferation Violations** (IAEA Resolutions, UNSC Resolutions, and the relevant Treaties/Agreements), **Systematic Crimes Against Humanity** (UNSC Resolutions, the relevant Treaties, and G.A. Resolutions) and **Human Rights Violations** (All relevant Treaties/Agreements). The second and third reports illustrate a detailed picture about the diverse categories and statistics of human rights violations, such as crackdown of freedom defenders, ethnic minorities' activists, religious converts, etc. in different provinces of Iran. **Existence of a Subcommittee dedicated to the grave systematic human rights abuses in Iran would be of great help in this regard, and bring rays of hope to the Iranians again.**

A First Project on the Subcommittee's Docket: Satellite Signal Jamming

In addition to the grave systematic violations of fundamental human rights mentioned in the above reports, there are other cases of human rights abuses in Iran. Mention, *inter alia*, can be made of censorship and prevention of free flow of information through extensive **orbital and terrestrial satellite jamming** and internet filtering. This censorship is a **violation of Article 15 of the Radio Regulations of the International**

Telecommunications Union and, more importantly, a blatant **violation of Article 19 of the Universal Declaration of Human Rights** that stipulates, "Everyone has the right to freedom of opinion and expression; this right includes freedom to hold opinions without interference and to seek, receive and impart information and ideas through any media and regardless of frontiers."

Moreover, the Iranian regime is accused of exposing their people to severe jamming signals which are said to be harmful to human body. The extent of **adverse medical effects of jamming signals** on the Iranian people is not clear since the Iranian authorities have never divulged the exact strength of the frequencies used to jam signals. However, some Iranian health organizations' experts have given warnings, and even some Iranian officials and government institutions have confessed, about the negative health impacts caused by jamming: dizziness, chronic deafness, and different kinds of cancer such as skin cancer, blood cancer, and marrow cancer, as well as impact on human hormones which could lead to infertility.[1]

The Iranian government continues to send jamming signals. **It is hereby suggested that the said Standing Subcommittee work on the ways to exert pressure on the Iranian regime to stop sending jamming signals.** This would not only be sending a clear message of care by the US to the Iranian people, but it would also help the free flow of information, as a human right, in Iran to tremendously help the freedom defenders and opposition groups in their cause.

A Second Project on the Subcommittee's Docket: Human Rights Abuse Finances

Pursuant to the recent Joint Plan of Action, adopted in Geneva on Nov 24, 2013, and the extension thereof, by the 5+1 and Iran, and the probable final agreement to be reached between the two sides, it is expected that a considerable portion of Iran's money be released. Given the fact that the Iranian regime has a long history of using their **financial resources to fund its extensive violation of human rights** (through purchase of equipment and hefty payments to its agents)**, and to sponsor terrorism and terrorist organizations, it would be advisable for the Subcommittee to work on policies for the release of the money in a way to ensure the money would not be used for those illegitimate and illegal purposes,** albeit with full control on the transactions by Iran.

---

[1] http://20ist.com/archives/12802
http://www.ebtekarnews.com/Ebtekar/News.aspx?NID=61505
http://parianet.blogsky.com/1390/01/19/post-4
http://www.tabnak.ir/fa/news/305623/%D9%BE%D8%B1%D8%AA%D9%88%D9%87%D8%A7-%D8%AF%D9%88%D9%85%DB%8C%D9%86-%D8%B9%D8%A7%D9%85%D9%84-%D8%B3%D8%B1%D8%B7%D8%A7%D9%86-%D8%B2%D8%A7-%D8%A7%D8%B3%D8%AA
http://www.ghatreh.com/news/nn11250897/%D8%B9%D9%88%D8%A7%D8%B1%D8%B6-%D9%BE%D8%A7%D8%B1%D8%A7%D8%B2%DB%8C%D8%AA-%D8%B3%D9%84%D8%A7%D9%85%D8%AA-%D9%85%D8%B1%D8%AF%D9%85

It is also noteworthy that the vast majority of the Iranian people are tired of seeing "their money being wasted in other countries or are used against the Iranian men and women". Control over where and how the Iranian people's money is spent would create optimism about the US policy against the ruling regime and bring hope among the Iranian people that their money would not sink in the sands of corruption and terrorism sponsorship, or be used to suppress them.

The Said Subcommittee may conclude than adoption of this policy would not even require any new legislation in the US. The following provisions would render adequate legislation for the US government to maintain its control in this regard:

- "Uniting and Strengthening America by Providing Appropriate Tools Required to Intercept and Obstruct Terrorism (USA PATRIOT ACT) Act of 2001", HR 3162: especially Section 330 of Title III of the Act concerning international cooperation in investigations of money laundering, financial crimes, and the finances of terrorist groups
- "Nuclear Iran Prevention Act of 2013", HR 850: particularly Titles I (Sections 101 – 103) and Title II (Sections 202 & 203) therein concerning "Human rights and Terrorism Sanctions" and "Economic and Financial Sanctions"
- Government decrees and Executive Orders such as E.O. 13553 and E.O. 13606
- Other financial anti-terrorist legislation

Provision of a control mechanism over Iran's financial transaction is also in compliance with the item in the "Joint Plan of Action" (JPA) reading "Establish a financial channel to facilitate humanitarian trade for Iran's domestic needs using Iranian oil revenues held abroad". The Iranian government is familiar with this concept, is in the position of breaking point, and will undoubtedly accept such mechanisms provided that it is insisted on in the negotiations. **The Standing Subcommittee can play a key role in reviewing this important leverage to help stop or at least mitigate violation of human rights in Iran.**